also by

COLETTE PETERS

COLETTE'S CAKES

COLETTE'S CHRISTMAS

COLETTE'S WEDDING CAKES

Colette's
birthday cakes

COLETTE PETERS

LITTLE, BROWN AND COMPANY

BOSTON NEW YORK LONDON

FIRST EDITION

Library of Congress Cataloging-in-Publication Data

Peters, Colette.

Colette's birthday cakes / Colette Peters.—1st ed.

p.   cm.

includes index.

ISBN 0-316-70274-9 (hc)

1. Cake decorating.   2. Birthday cakes.   I. Title.

TX771.2.P46 2000

641.8'653—dc21   99-36425

10   9   8   7   6   5   4   3

RRD-RVA

Printed in the United States of America

contents

I would like to thank everyone who helped me with this book.
I couldn't have done it without you!

Amy Loughlin, Ryan "Sudsy" Hurley, Margot Abel,
Ellen Silverman, Kerry McGrath, Marina Malchin, James Couto,
Karlyn Donahoe, Barbara Arvanitis, Victoria Love,
Carol Falcone, Terry Kotek, Jennifer Josephy,
and last but not least Arlene Bluth.

introduction

Birthdays are a delight the whole world shares: not only do we all have one, we all have one *every year!* In my profession, making custom cakes for all occasions, I've become aware, over the years, of just how significant birthdays can be. From bar and bat mitzvahs to parties for eighty-year-olds, birthdays make up more than two-thirds of my business.

Since the days when only kings had public birthday celebrations, virtually every culture has bestowed this special day with its own customs and traditions. Many of these were meant to bring luck, which still plays an important role in our own festivities. Long ago, people believed that being closely surrounded by well-wishers on one's birthday would dispel evil spirits; today we make a wish and blow out the birthday candles in a single breath, for luck. Astrology, mapping out the powerful influence of the zodiac signs under which we are born, is another popular belief system that links our birthdays to our destinies. And each month also has a birthstone and flower that symbolize good luck and prosperity for anyone born during that time.

In the United States and many other countries, one of the most cherished traditions is the birthday cake. Its origin is not conclusively known. One theory holds that round cakes, aglow with candles, once honored Artemis, the Greek goddess of the moon. Another suggests that birthday cakes with candles originated in Germany several centuries ago, along with *kinderfesten* (children's birthday parties). Whatever its genesis, whether you celebrate with a huge party or with just a few of your nearest and dearest, it's hard to imagine a birthday without a cake.

What I love best about birthdays is that they are an occasion when friends and families come together, not only to mark someone's passage through life but also to pay tribute to that person's uniqueness. And, of course, to eat cake! As a cake designer, I have the fun of creating one-of-a-kind cakes for a loved one's special day, and of sharing in the celebration by learning about his or her likes, fantasies, and accomplishments. My customers often reveal to me many intimate details about the life of the person they wish to celebrate. I feel I know them even when I haven't met them. The challenge is always to design a cake incorporating important aspects of the person's life in a creative and visual way.

In this book, I have included cakes that are appropriate for different ages, sexes, and styles. For the decorator, I've introduced techniques of varying degrees of difficulty. More than anything else, I want these cakes to be as enjoyable to make as they will be to serve. About a third of the cakes are based on individuals' professional or personal interests, and include some I have made for my friends and even myself. The rest are grouped by astrological signs, flowers of the month, and birthstones, which are listed here.

The best way to use this book is to read the chapters in the back entitled "Basic Recipes" and "Basic Instructions" before you begin. These chapters explain the techniques, tools, and materials you will need, as well as how to make the decorations and assemble the cakes. Rely on them for general reference as you follow the directions for individual cakes. The "Basic Recipes" section contains instructions for making cakes, rolled fondant, and various icings, along with a chart to help you determine how much fondant you will need to cover a given cake. The amount of icing required for each cake will depend on whether you plan to use it for filling, icing, or decorating, so the directions do not specify quantities. When you make your cake, keep a supply of icing ingredients on hand so you can make more as you need it.

Finally, there are a few other ingredients essential to any birthday celebration that you won't find listed anywhere in the recipes: fun, a feeling of togetherness, and lots of creativity!

Signs of the Zodiac

Aquarius	January 20–February 18
Pisces	February 19–March 20
Aries	March 21–April 19
Taurus	April 20–May 20
Gemini	May 21–June 21
Cancer	June 22–July 22
Leo	July 23–August 22
Virgo	August 23–September 22
Libra	September 23–October 23
Scorpio	October 24–November 22
Sagittarius	November 23–December 21
Capricorn	December 22–January 19

Month	Flower	Birthstone
January	snowdrop	garnet
February	violet	amethyst
March	jonquil	aquamarine
April	daisy	diamond
May	lily of the valley	emerald
June	rose	pearl
July	water lily	ruby
August	poppy	peridot
September	morning glory	sapphire
October	marigold	opal
November	chrysanthemum	topaz
December	narcissus and holly	turquoise

signs of

the

zodiac

the water pitcher

SERVES 60

To celebrate the birthday of an Aquarius, the zodiac sign whose symbol is the water bearer, I created a mosaic pitcher made of fondant, with spilling water fashioned in piping gel.

- cakes:
  3 13-by-9⅞-inch ovals,
  each 2 inches high
- 2 13-by-9⅞-inch oval
  foamcore boards
- 3 20-inch-wide foamcore
  boards for base
- 1-inch-thick roll of masking tape
- X-acto knife
- white glue
- royal icing (page 147)
- ³⁄₁₆-inch-wide white
  ribbon
- rolled fondant (page 145)
- S-shaped crimper
- 20 #20-gauge white
  cloth-covered wires,
  18 inches long
- pastry bags and couplers
- tip: PME #2
- colors:
- blue liquid food coloring
- blue, rose, green, brown,
  and teal nontoxic airbrush
  paint

- blue nontoxic iridescent
  powder
- caramel, eggshell, purple,
  blue, flesh, pale-green,
  royal-blue, and sky-blue
  paste
- clear piping gel
- block of Styrofoam for
  drying
- small serrated knife
- airbrush (page 171)
- smooth tracing wheel
- blue nontoxic felt-tip
  marker
- lemon extract
- small paintbrush
- pizza cutter

In advance:

Cut the smaller foamcore ovals as directed in the section on cake bases (page 175). For the 3-tiered cake base, trace the outline of the cake pan on one of the boards, then use the roll of masking tape to enlarge the oval by 1 inch all around (see page 175), and cut out the larger oval with the X-acto knife. Make the next oval using the first board and the roll of masking tape as before, then make the third board using the second board and the tape.

To assemble the stepped cake base, stack the 3 oval boards, centered, and glue them together, placing something heavy on top to keep them flat while they dry. Cover the boards with thinned white royal icing and let dry. Attach cords of fondant around the stepped edges of the base with a little water and emboss continuous borders with the S-shaped crimper. Glue the ribbon around the bottom foamcore edge.

To make the gel-covered wires, bend each wire into a curlicue, leaving one end uncurled. Hold the wire upright by its straight end as you pipe.

3

Using the #2 tip, pipe beads of clear piping gel down one side of the wire (**1**). Stop at least 2 inches above the end you're holding, so you can insert the wire into the cake. Now pipe down the other side, using light-blue piping gel. Insert the wires in a block of Styrofoam to dry, taking care not to let them touch one another.

To decorate:

Bake the cakes and let them cool completely. Place the tiers on their corresponding boards and fill them. There will be a foamcore separation 3 inches up from the bottom (for instructions, see the section on constructing tiered cakes, page 150). Stack the layers together and, using the serrated knife, cut away the top so the cake slopes from 6 inches high at one end to 4 inches high at the other. Carefully shave off the top of the cake until it is slightly curved and forms the shape of the pitcher (**2** and **3**).

Crumb-coat the cake (see page 150) and chill. Cover it with beige fondant made with the caramel paste color. Airbrush the bottom of the cake and the base light blue (see page 171). With the tracing wheel, score the sides of the cake with curved lines as shown in figure **2**. Using a blue nontoxic marking pen, color in these lines. Mix blue iridescent powder with lemon extract and paint the cake and the tops of the crimped borders on the base.

Roll out a piece of eggshell-colored fondant ⅛ inch thick and large enough to fit the flower and bow patterns (**4**, **5**, and **6**). Cut out the insides of the patterns to make stencils. Place the stencils on the piece of fondant and airbrush the flowers and the bow pink and the leaves green. Brush-embroider the designs with white royal icing (see page 147). While the icing is still wet, cut up the designs into small pieces with the pizza cutter. Let the royal icing dry. Transfer the fondant pieces to the cake as shown in the photograph on page 2, attaching them with a little royal icing. Now cut two 9-by-1½-inch strips of fondant. Make a stencil out of the border pattern (**7**), place it on the fondant, and airbrush the strips green. Cut them into small squares and transfer them to the cake as shown in the photograph, attaching them with royal icing. Attach the pieces on both sides of the bow design and at the bottom edge of the pitcher.

Fill in the surface of the top tier with irregular-shaped "tiles" cut from eggshell fondant, interspersed with individual tiles of purple, light blue and dark blue, pale green, flesh, and beige. For the mouth of the pitcher, use rows of flesh, dark blue, light blue, and beige; for the bottom, use beige topped with a narrow strip of flesh-colored pieces. Around the base of the cake, alternate purple, light-blue, and dark-blue tiles.

For the handles, roll two 6-inch-long coils of eggshell fondant, each ¾ inch thick and tapered at one end. Shape the coils into curved handles and place them on each side of the pitcher, on the curved part of the bottom tier. Attach the thicker ends to the pitcher's neck, using royal icing.

Insert the wires into the top tier around the mouth of the pitcher.

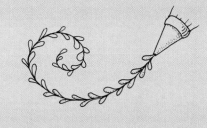

1

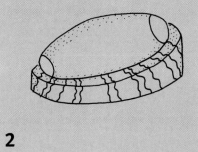

2

3

4 enlarge 164%

5 enlarge 194%

6 enlarge 175%

7 enlarge 150%

the deep blue sea

SERVES 80

Schools of colorful fish made of fondant and gum paste swirl around this five-tiered cake designed for a Pisces birthday. To support the taller tiers, two decorated layers of Styrofoam serve as cakes in disguise.

In advance:

Make the gum-paste fish. Tint some gum paste blue and some coral and shape the gum-paste fish (see the photograph on page 9), using the veining tool to add detail. Emboss the scales with the #81 tip. Let dry overnight. Mix green pearl iridescent powder with lemon extract and paint the blue fish. Mix orange iridescent powder with lemon extract and paint the coral fish.

Using the run-in-sugar technique (see page 170), outline and fill in 3 fish on wires with royal icing. Let dry. Repeat on back. Let dry. Mix orange iridescent powder with lemon extract and paint one fish and the top half of another. Mix green pearl and super pearl iridescent powder with lemon extract and paint the third fish and the bottom half of the second fish.

Cover the foil base with thinned blue royal icing. Let dry.

To decorate:

Bake the cakes and let them cool completely. Fill the tiers and assemble them on their correspon-

- cakes:
- – 6-inch petal,
  4 inches high
- – 10-inch petal,
  1½ inches high
- – 12-inch petal,
  4 inches high
- gum paste (page 154)
- colors:
- – blue, coral, moss-green,
  and yellow paste
- – nontoxic green pearl,
  super pearl, and orange
  iridescent powder
- – blue airbrush paint
- gum-paste veining tool
- pastry bags and couplers
- tips: #81, PME #2, PME #3
- lemon extract
- paintbrushes
- 3 #24-gauge white
  cloth-covered wires,
  7 inches long
- royal icing (page 147)
- 16-inch round foil-covered
  base, ½ inch high

- 6-, 10-, and 12-inch petal
  foamcore boards
- 5-inch petal Styrofoam,
  1 inch high, with a petal
  foamcore board attached
- 10-inch petal Styrofoam,
  3½ inches high, with
  a petal foamcore board
  attached
- rolled fondant (page 145)
- ¼-inch-thick wooden
  dowels
- airbrush
- JEM slanted scallop and
  broad scallop ruffle cutters, assorted cutters for
  fish (see page 9)

ding foamcore boards. Crumb-coat all the cake tiers (see page 150) and chill them. Cover all the tiers with blue rolled fondant. Rub the Styrofoam tiers with water and cover them, too. Center the 10-inch Styrofoam tier on the base, attaching it with royal icing. Insert dowels in the 10- and 12-inch tiers.

Roll out some of the blue fondant ⅛ inch thick. Using pattern **1**, cut out 18 fish and tails. Brush their backs with a little water and attach them in a row around the bottom border of the 10-inch Styrofoam tier. Roll out a piece of coral fondant and, using pattern **2**, cut out 32 fish and tails. Attach these about halfway up the side of the tier in a wavy line, facing the opposite way from the fish below. Emboss eyes on all of the fish using the #2 tip.

Stack the 12-inch cake tier centered on the Styrofoam tier and attach it with royal icing. Then center and attach the 10-inch cake tier. Cut out 18 more blue fondant fish and attach them, facing in the same direction as the first row on the tier below, around the bottom of the 10-inch cake layer. Stack the 5-inch Styrofoam and then the 6-inch cake. Using the airbrush, spray the cake and the base with blue, making the color darker at the top of the tiers and gradually lighter down the sides.

Tint some fondant pale green and use pattern **3** to cut out 15 fish. Attach these in a row around the bottom of the 5-inch Styrofoam layer. Roll out some blue fondant ⅛ inch thick. Using the ruffle cutters and patterns **4** and **5**, cut ruffles for the 6-inch and 12-inch tiers. Brush a little water along the straight edges of the cutouts to attach them to the bottom edges of the tiers.

Using patterns **2** and **3**, cut out 21 fish and fish tails and attach them to the ruffle on the 12-inch tier, as shown in the photograph on page 9. Place the larger fish facing left and the smaller ones above, facing right.

Tint some fondant pale orange and use figure **6** to cut out 70 fish. Attach them to the cake as follows: 25 on the top tier, 10 around the middle, 20 on the bottom tier, and 15 on the base. Let some of the tails curve, and let others rotate out away from the surface of the cake.

With a #2 tip and blue royal icing, outline the ruffle and pipe a snail trail along the top edge. Pipe dots along the bottoms of the tiers around the blue fish. Pipe larger and smaller dots around the base and the tiers to resemble bubbles. Pipe a curved line for gills near the head of the fish on the 10-inch tier.

Mix green pearl iridescent powder with lemon extract and brush it on the green and blue fish and on some of the bubbles on the bottom half of the cake. Mix orange iridescent powder with lemon extract and brush it on the blue fish on the 10-inch tier and on all the orange fish. Insert the wired royal-icing fish into the 10- and 12-inch tiers. Attach the gum-paste decorations to the top of the cake using royal icing.

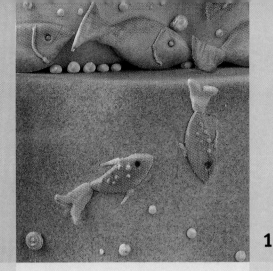

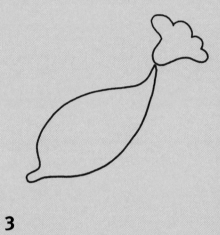

1

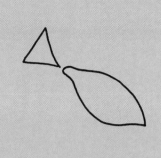

2

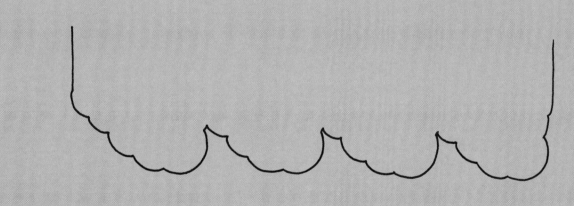

3

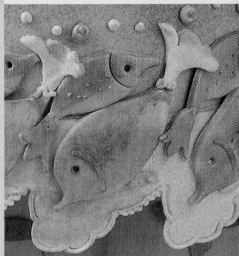

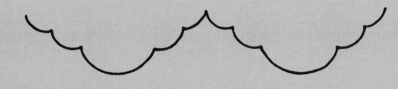

4

5

6

antique velvet purse

(ARIES)

1

SERVES 12

The decorations on this cake are based on a style of embroidery popular in seventeenth-century England — the fine stitching known as stumpwork. The symbol of Aries, the horned ram, is incorporated into the metalwork design of the purse's clasp.

In advance:

Enlarge pattern **1** by 210 percent, trace it on the foamcore board, and cut out the shape using the X-acto knife.

Place the metalwork pattern (**2**) on a cookie sheet and tape a sheet of wax or parchment paper over it. Using the #7 tip, pipe the pattern onto the paper with slightly thinned royal icing.

To make the chain handle, roll a cord of gum paste ¼ inch in diameter and 2 inches long. Wet the ends and press them together to form a ring. Roll another cord, pass it through the center of the first ring, then press the ends of the second link together (**3**). Repeat until the chain is 21 inches long. Let it dry on a cookie sheet for 24 hours.

To decorate:

Bake the cake and let it cool completely. Fill the layers, assemble them, and place the foamcore

- cake:
  8-inch round, 2½ inches high
- 8-inch round foamcore board
- X-acto knife
- wax paper or silicone-coated parchment paper
- pastry bags and couplers
- tips: #7, PME #2
- royal icing (page 147)
- gum paste (page 154)
- serrated knife
- rolled fondant (page 145)
- gum-paste veining tool
- cocoa powder

- colors:
  - moss-green, red, rose, brown, and violet paste
  - nontoxic light-blue, super pearl, and gold iridescent powders
- tracing wheel
- lemon extract
- small paintbrush
- clear piping gel

board on top. Using the serrated knife, shave off the edges of the cake in the shape of the board. Remove the board, crumb-coat the cake (see page 150), and chill it. Cover the cake with chocolate fondant, gathering the icing together at the narrower end — the top of the "purse" — to make folds (**4**). Use the veining tool to press in the fondant at the folds and exaggerate them. Dust the cake with cocoa powder to achieve a matte finish resembling the look of old velvet.

Using the #2 tip and green royal icing, pipe the stitched pattern (**5**) over the cake. Overpipe the edges of the leaves (see page 152).

To make the dragonfly: Using figure **5** as a guide, roll small amounts of white fondant into small balls for the body and the eyes. Attach them to the cake with a little water. Pipe the outline of the wings and their inner design with the #2 tip and white royal icing. Paint the inside of the wings with super pearl mixed with lemon extract.

To make the carnation: Using figure **6** as a guide, pipe the base of the flower with green royal icing, using a back-and-forth motion. Cut the 4 petals out of rose-colored fondant with a small knife and emboss the tiny dots inside each one with the veining tool. Attach the petals above the base with a little water. Pipe 3 small dots on the top of each petal with rose-colored icing. Then pipe a green calyx at the base of each petal.

To make the currants: Roll 6 small balls of light-brown fondant and attach them to the cake in a small cluster, using a little water (**7**). Emboss a small hole in the center of each berry, then pipe a dot of white royal icing in the holes.

To make the thistles: Roll 2 small balls of light-brown fondant, one slightly larger than the other, and flatten the top of each (**8**). Attach them to the ends of the stems with a little water.

Using the tracing wheel, make criss-cross dotted lines on each. Then, using violet royal icing and the #2 tip, pipe thin lines coming out of the flat top of the base for the petals. Pipe 3 green dots at the base of each flower.

To make the strawberry: Form a cone-shaped piece of light-brown fondant and attach it to the end of the stem (**9**). Using the veining tool, press small holes into the berry. Pipe 3 green calyxes at the base with the #2 tip.

To make the raspberries: Pipe small clusters of red royal-icing dots at the ends of 2 stems, using the #2 tip (see photograph on page 13). When the red icing is dry, paint with clear piping gel. Pipe 3 small calyxes at the base of each cluster using green royal icing and the #2 tip.

To make the rest of the berries, pipe dots of rose royal icing at the base of the stems using the #2 tip. Pipe small violet dots as shown in figure **10**.

Paint the dragonfly, the centers of the currants, and the base of the carnation with light-blue iridescent powdered color mixed with lemon extract.

Mix gold iridescent powder with lemon extract and paint the metalwork pattern and the gum-paste chain. Attach the metalwork to the narrower end of the cake with royal icing and prop it up until it dries. Fasten the chain to both ends of the cake using royal icing. Prop it in place until it is completely dry.

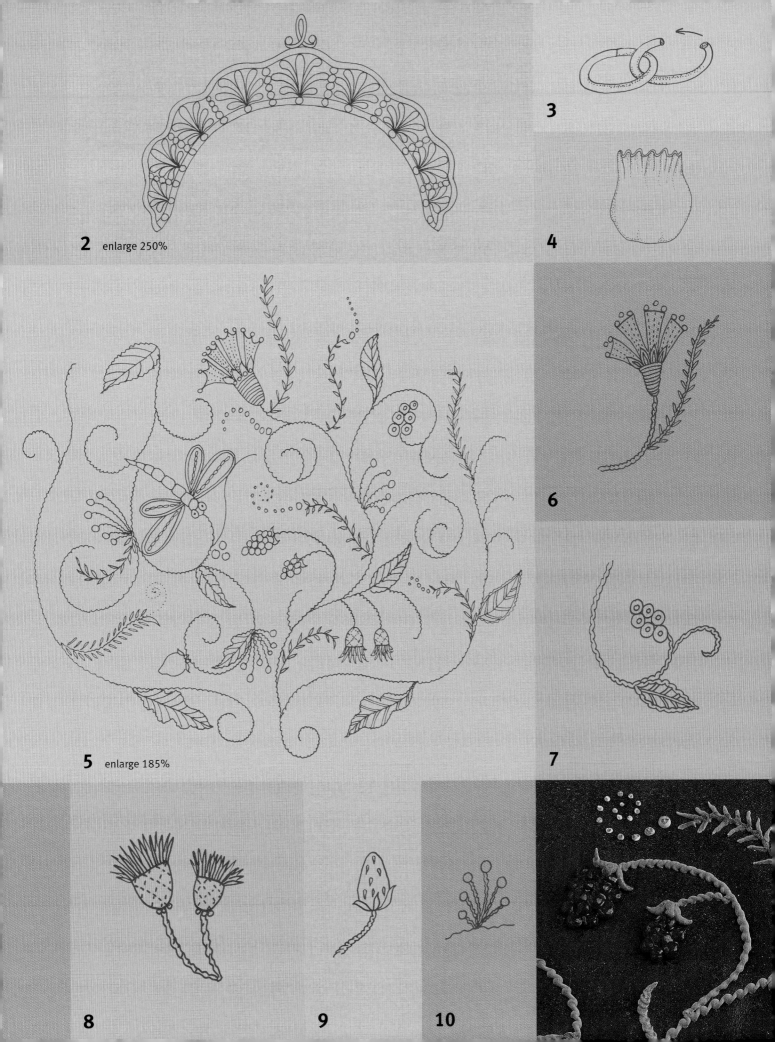

2 enlarge 250%

3

4

5 enlarge 185%

6

7

8

9

10

just deserts

SERVES 40

For this Taurus cake, I looked to the paintings of Georgia O'Keeffe for inspiration. Where O'Keeffe saw the austere beauty of the desert, I see . . . dessert! In this sweet landscape, the skull is the cake, the sand is sugar, and the rattlesnake, cacti, and rocks are cookies.

In advance:

Enlarge pattern **1** by 200 percent, trace it on the foamcore board, and cut out the shape with the X-acto knife.

Make the Rice Krispies Treats recipe and chill the mixture for 5 minutes. When the mixture is stiff, shape the horns with your hand, squeezing them until they are firmly packed. The horns should be 10½ inches long, with a 2½-by-1½-inch oval base (see figure **2** for the shape). Insert a skewer into the bottom of each horn as far as it will go, leaving about 3 inches of the stick showing. Insert the skewers into the block of Styrofoam and let the horns harden. Tint some royal icing with a mixture of lemon-yellow and a tiny bit of violet coloring. Thin the icing to the consistency of corn syrup and paint the horns, using a wet paintbrush to smooth away the brushstrokes. Let dry and repeat until the horns are smooth.

- cake:
  13-by-9½-inch,
  4½ inches high
- 14-inch-square foamcore board
- X-acto knife
- 1 recipe Rice Krispies Treats (found on boxes of Rice Krispies cereal)
- wooden skewers
- block of Styrofoam
- royal icing (page 147)
- colors:
- lemon-yellow, violet, moss-green, kelly-green, willow-green, leaf-green, orange, red, brown, and caramel paste
- nontoxic black powder

- paintbrush
- Desert Cookies (page 148)
- rolling pin
- sharp knife
- pastry bags and couplers
- tips: PME #2, PME #3
- palette knife
- ivory rolled fondant (page 145)

Roll out the cookie dough. Trace patterns **3–11** on sheets of paper and cut them out. Place the patterns on top of the dough and cut out the cookies with a sharp knife. Bake them as directed on page 148 and let them cool completely. Decorate the cookies using the run-in-sugar technique. Outline the cactus stems and flowers and the snake's markings, using royal icing and the #3 tip. Fill the cacti with a variety of greens, using the photos as a guide. Use thinned royal icing, and the #2 tip, as on page 17. Overpipe where indicated. To make the cactus spines and the centers of the flowers, pipe pale yellow dots and then pull the tip up from the surface. To decorate the rocks, use small amounts of brown, black, and dark-green royal icing. Spread the three colors with a palette knife to create a marbled effect.

To decorate:

Bake the cake and let it cool completely. Fill the layers and assemble them. Place the board on top. Using the serrated knife, carve the cake a little at a time, following the outline of the board. Invert the cake and the board and continue carving the shape of a steer skull (**1**). Crumb-coat the cake (see page 150) and chill it. Cover the cake with ivory rolled fondant. Press the fondant into the cavities of the eyes and nose and use the knife to make the bone indentations.

Insert the skewers on the end of the horns into the cake and glue the horns to the cake using ivory royal icing. Dust the eye sockets and the nasal cavity with black powdered color. Brush black powder over the indented lines and wipe off any excess powder with a clean, damp cloth to give the surface a "bonelike" finish.

1

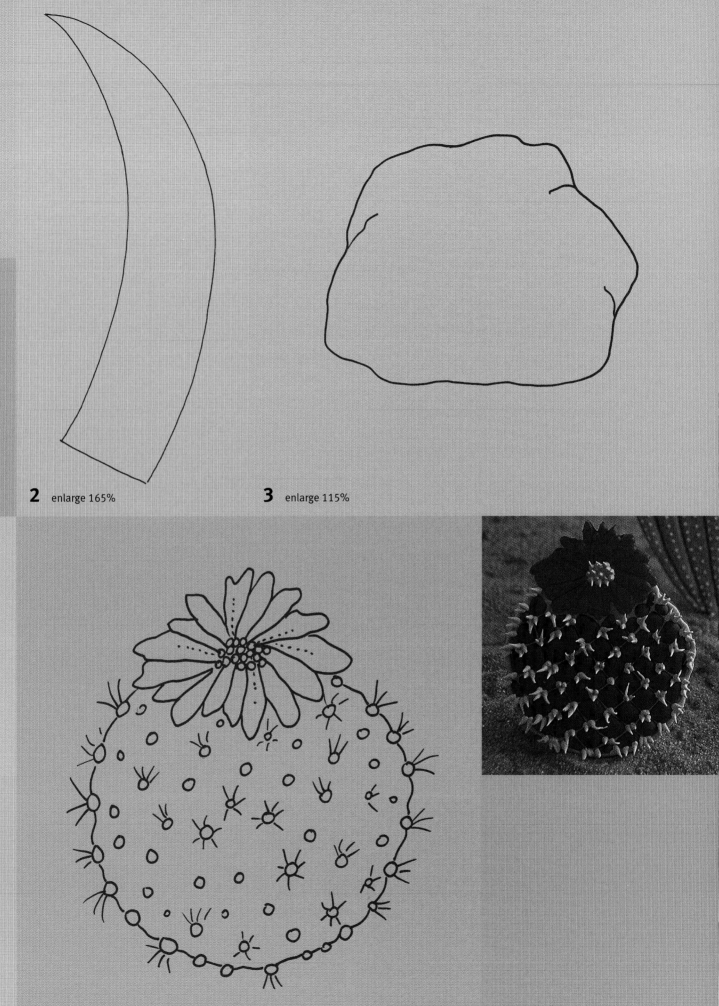

2 enlarge 165%

3 enlarge 115%

4 enlarge 115%

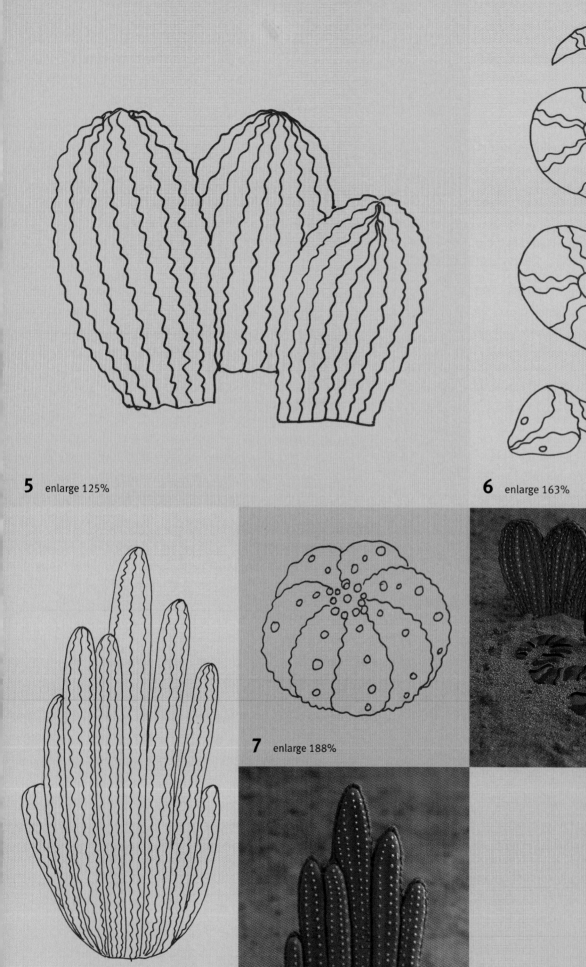

5 enlarge 125%

6 enlarge 163%

7 enlarge 188%

8 enlarge 225%

9 enlarge 177%

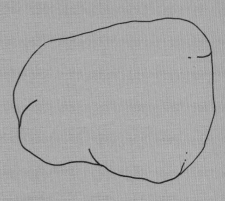

10 enlarge 178%

11 enlarge 185%

à deux

SERVES 50

For Gemini, the sign of the twins, I envisioned two feminine faces surrounded by cascading hair. You can use a silicone mold for the faces (see "Sources" for mail-order information), or you can simply sculpt them in fondant — a great opportunity to give free rein to your artistry and imagination.

- cake:
  14-inch square,
  3 inches high
- 1 14-inch- and 2 18-inch-square foamcore boards
- X-acto knife
- 2-inch-thick roll of masking tape
- white glue
- royal icing (page 147)
- paintbrush
- colors:
- caramel paste
- nontoxic brown and pink powder
- gum paste (page 154)
- small rolling pin
- variety of flower and leaf cutters (pages 167–169)
- tracing wheel
- gum-paste ball and veining tools
- white and pink stamens
- pastry bags and couplers
- tip: PME #3
- small serrated knife
- silicone mold (optional)
- rolled fondant (page 145)
- potato ricer or clay gun (optional)

In advance:

Enlarge pattern **1** by 230 percent, trace it on the 14-inch foamcore board, and cut out the shape with the X-acto knife. Then cut one of the 18-inch boards, using the smaller board as a template and enlarging the shape on all sides with the roll of masking tape (see the section on cake bases, page 175). Glue the larger cut board to the remaining 18-inch board, placing something heavy on top to keep the boards flat while they dry. When the boards are dry, cut the square board to match the other.

Cover the base with thinned white royal icing.

Tint some gum paste ivory (made with caramel coloring) and leave some white. Roll out some of the gum paste ⅛ inch thick and use the cutters to make a variety of flowers, layering white cutouts with ivory ones. Use your imagination to create

21

unusual combinations of fantasy flowers and leaves (**2**–**4**). Emboss some of the petals and leaves with the tracing wheel and various gum-paste tools. With the #3 tip, pipe centers with white royal icing and insert white or pink stamens. Let dry.

To decorate:

Bake the cake and let it cool completely. Fill the layers, assemble them, and place the 14-inch board on top. Use the serrated knife to cut off the sides of the cake a little at a time in the shape of the board. Attach the cake to the board with a little icing. Crumb-coat the cake (see page 150) and chill it. Cover the cake with white rolled fondant. With the veining tool, score the fondant on the side of the cake horizontally all around so that it has the texture of hair.

To sculpt the faces, I made a silicone mold, which can be purchased from me (see "Sources"). You can also shape them from fondant, which is very pliable when fresh. Place some fondant directly on top of the cake and form the features, using pattern **5** and the photograph on page 20 as a guide. Use the veining tool to emboss the eyes, brows, nostrils, and lips.

Dust the skin lightly with powdered color to achieve a natural tone, just as you would apply makeup. Mix brown powdered color with water to paint the eyes, brows, and lashes and to shade the nostrils. Paint the lips pink, building from a lighter shade to a darker one at the edges.

The cords of fondant for the hair can be rolled by hand ¼ inch thick or pressed through the ⅜-inch-circle of a clay gun. I made them by pushing the fondant through a potato ricer, but if you don't have access to one, the just-mentioned alternatives will do nicely. Attach the coils at the crowns of the heads with a little water, curling them around the faces and the sides of the cake.

Attach the flowers to the cake with royal icing.

1

2

3

4

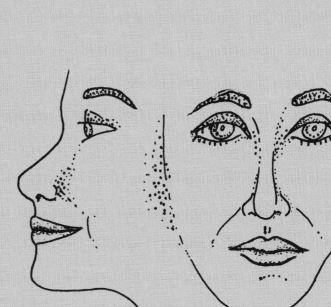

5 enlarge 168%

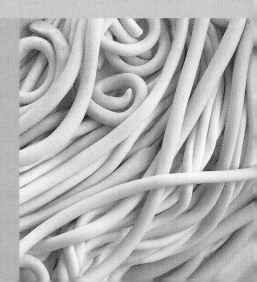

crab cake

SERVES 50 Cancer's symbol is the crab, a creature not normally associated with sweets. For a real birthday surprise, make this amusing cake for the crabs in your life.

In advance:

Cover the base with thinned orange royal icing and let it dry. Glue the ribbon around the edge, or leave the foil exposed. For the crab's eyes, roll out 2 small pieces of gum paste, each 2 inches long, with a slightly larger ball at one end. Let dry.

To decorate:

Bake the cake and let it cool completely. Fill the cake and assemble it on the board. Trace pattern **1**, for the crab's legs and claws, on a sheet of paper and enlarge it by 240 percent. Place the paper at one edge of the cake and score the outline with the tip of the knife. Turn the paper over and repeat on the opposite edge of the cake. Working in from the edge, carefully shave the cake a little at a time to form the legs and claws. The top surface of the cake should be slightly curved. Crumb-coat the cake (see page 150) and chill it.

Cover the cake with orange fondant and attach it to the base with royal icing. Add more fondant to the outside of the claws to enlarge them.

- cake:
  12-inch round,
  3 inches high
- 16-inch round base,
  ½ inch high
- royal icing (page 147)
- colors:
- orange paste
- yellow, orange, and brown airbrush paint
- ½-inch-wide orange ribbon (optional)
- white glue (optional)
- gum paste (page 154)
- 12-inch round foamcore board
- small serrated knife
- rolled fondant (page 145)
- gum-paste veining tool
- airbrush

Using the photograph on page 24 as a guide, emboss the details with the veining tool, shaping the mouth and the inside of the claws with zigzag lines.

Enhance the colors and details with the airbrush, starting with yellow, then switching to orange and finally brown. After applying each layer, while it is still wet, blot it with a paper towel to create a mottled look. As a finishing touch, add the dark spots by holding the nozzle of the airbrush very close to the surface of the cake. This will create a ring of brown around an uncolored center. Make 2 small holes above the mouth and insert the gum-paste eyes.

1

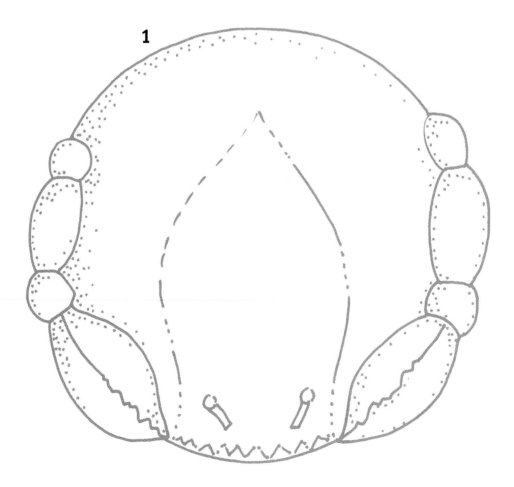

leo
the lovable
lion

(LEO)

SERVES 50 The inspiration for this cake came from a book about paper sculpture: I thought adapting some of the same techniques for cake decorating would be both challenging and fun. The lion's mane, made of modeling chocolate, is based on the art of paper filigree, called quilling.

1

In advance:

Cover the base with thinned brown royal icing. Let dry. Glue the ribbon around the edge.

Enlarge pattern **1** by 200 percent and place it on the foamcore board. Cut out the shape with an X-acto knife.

Make the 5 different colors of modeling chocolate and let them set overnight, wrapped separately in plastic wrap. Add white to the yellow and orange to lighten them. Flatten pieces of the chocolate with the heel of your hand and run them through the pasta machine, starting at the widest opening (#1) and progressing through the smaller ones, ending with #4. If you don't have a pasta machine, just roll each piece out to ⅛ inch thick with a rolling pin.

With the straightedge serving as a template, use the pizza cutter to cut the chocolate into ¾-inch-wide strips of various lengths, ranging from 3 to 5 inches. Bend them into curled shapes as

- cake:
  12-inch square,
  4 inches high
- 16-inch round base,
  ½ inch high
- royal icing (page 147)
- colors:
- brown paste
- nontoxic brown powder
- ½-inch-wide orange ribbon
- white glue
- 12-inch-square foamcore board
- X-acto knife
- modeling chocolate (page 144) made with light and dark cocoa and orange, yellow, and white confectionery coating

- pasta machine (optional) or rolling pin
- ¾-inch-wide straightedge
- pizza cutter
- rolled fondant (page 145)
- tips: #4, #8
- lemon extract
- small paintbrush
- clay gun
- clear piping gel

7

shown in the photograph on page 29. Let them stand on their sides on a cookie sheet to set.

To decorate:

Bake the cake and let it cool completely. Fill the cake layers and assemble them. Place the foam-core board on top. Using the serrated knife, cut away the sides of the cake a little at a time to match the shape of the board. Place the cake on the board. Carve the lion's head, shaving away the shaded areas at the top to form the face, using pattern **2** (enlarged by 133 percent) as an outline. Crumb-coat the cake (see page 150) and chill it. Cover the cake with light-brown fondant and attach it to the base with royal icing.

Roll out another piece of light-brown fondant ⅛ inch thick. Enlarge pattern **2** by 133 percent, place it on top of the fondant, and cut out the lion's face with the pizza cutter. Carefully transfer the fondant face to the top of the cake, positioning it as shown in the photograph on page 29, and attach it with a little water after it is in place. Curl the top edges over to make the ears, and prop up the ears and the nose with pieces of paper towel until the fondant has set. Using pattern **2** as a guide, emboss the eyes by pressing the base of a #8 tip into the fondant. Emboss the pupils with the top of the tip and the whisker holes with the narrow end of the #4 tip.

Dust around the nose and inside the ears with brown powdered color. Mix brown powdered color with lemon extract and dab it with a paintbrush inside the ears and the eyes, leaving the pupils unpainted. Press dark-brown modeling chocolate through the ⅛-inch-circle die of the clay gun to outline the eyes, nose, whiskers, and mouth.

Working on one small area at a time, spread piping gel on the forehead, around the face,

and on the base where you want to attach the chocolate curls. Arrange the curls as shown in the photograph.

2

floral fan-tasy

SERVES 50

When I made this fan-shaped cake for my friend Diana's birthday, I based the design on passementerie, the intricate lace- and beadwork she loves to decorate her house with. Because Diana is a Virgo, I incorporated stalks of wheat, which represent her zodiac sign.

In advance:

To make the pattern for the gum-paste fan, draw the outline of the 20-inch cake pan on a large sheet of paper. Cut it out and fold it in half, then in quarters, then unfold it and cut it in half. Place one of the half-circles on a piece of lightweight cardboard and cut out the shape. Using the tape measure as a guide, mark the cardboard at 2-inch intervals along the half-circle's circumference, then draw lines from those marks to the circle's midpoint with the straightedge (**1**). Lightly score the lines with the tip of the X-acto knife and then fold up the cardboard like a fan. Open up the fan and tape it down onto a hard surface so that it won't collapse from the weight of the gum paste.

Roll out a piece of gum paste ⅛ inch thick and large enough to cover the cardboard. Place the half-circle paper pattern on top of the gum paste and cut along its outline with the pizza cutter. Using a compass, draw a 5-inch circle from the

- cake:
  20-inch round,
  2½ inches high
- sheet of paper at least
  20 by 20 inches
- lightweight cardboard
- straightedge
- tape measure
- serrated knife
- gum paste (page 154)
- X-acto knife
- pizza cutter
- 1¾-inch fluted biscuit
  cutter
- 10-by-20-inch foamcore
  board
- ¾-inch-wide
  Scotch Magic Tape
- airbrush
- colors:
- yellow, purple, copper,
  and flamingo-red airbrush
  paint
- nontoxic holly-green,
  mauve, and gold irides-
  cent powder

- green, mauve, caramel,
  rose, yellow, violet, black,
  and blue paste
- lemon extract
- paintbrushes
- royal icing (page 147)
- pastry bags and couplers
- tips: PME #2, PME #3
- wax paper
- 22-inch round base,
  ½ inch thick
- ½-inch-wide teal ribbon
- white glue
- rolled fondant (page 145)
- clay gun
- daisy cutter or Colette's
  medallion (see "Sources"
  on page 180)
- gum-paste umbrella tool

center point of the half-circle. Cut out the circle in the gum paste. Using the 1¾-inch biscuit cutter, cut out 9 arcs, each ½ inch deep, along the outer edge of the 5-inch circle of the gum paste (**2**). Drape the gum paste over the cardboard pattern, pressing it into the folds. Let dry for 2 days.

For the foamcore cake board, use the tape measure to mark a point on the other paper half-circle, 4 inches from one end (along the curved edge). Draw a line from this point to the circle's midpoint and cut along the line (**3**). Use the bigger segment as a template to cut the foamcore board.

Enlarge pattern **4** by 200 percent and cut out the overall shape. Go over the design with a number 2 pencil, pressing hard, then transfer the paper, design side down, onto the dried gum paste. Rub the back of the page with a pencil to transfer the design onto the gum paste.

Mask off a line along the top edge of the fan with ¾-inch-wide Scotch Magic Tape. Airbrush the fan, building the color from light to dark, starting with yellow, then adding a little purple, copper, and flamingo red. The center of the fan should be the lightest area, with the tone darkening toward the top. Let dry.

Carefully remove the tape. Mix holly-green iridescent powder with lemon extract and paint the exposed strip. Brush-embroider the larger leaves with green royal icing, the smaller leaves with pale-orange royal icing, made with yellow and rose, and the flowers with white royal icing. Paint the flowers with ocher, made with yellow, rose, and green, then mauve and beige, made with caramel. Using the #2 tip, outline the leaf veins with green royal icing and the smaller leaves with beige. Pipe dots of mauve icing in the centers of the flowers. Using the #3 tip, pipe the tendrils in rose icing. Using the #2 tip, pipe yellow icing around the fan's scalloped edge.

Carefully paint outlines around all of the flowers, leaves, and tendrils with a mixture of purple, flamingo-red, and copper airbrush color, using a small paintbrush.

Now make the ribs of the fan. Place pattern **5** under a sheet of wax paper taped to a baking sheet. Using the run-in-sugar technique (see page 170), outline and fill in 10 ribs with dark-violet (mixing black and violet) royal icing. Let dry. Create the wheat on the ribs and the border of the fan, as shown in the photograph on page 33, by piping dots and pulling them to a point in alternating directions.

Cover the base with thinned dark blue-green royal icing. Let dry. Glue the ribbon around the edge.

To decorate:

Bake the cake and let it cool completely. Cut the cake in half. Fill the layers and assemble them. Place the foamcore board on top. Using the serrated knife, cut the cake to match the shape of the board. Place the cake on the board, crumb-coat it (see page 150), and chill it. Cover the chilled cake with fondant. Mix mauve iridescent powder with lemon extract and paint the cake. Attach the cake to the center of the base with royal icing.

Remove the gum-paste fan from its cardboard support and place it on the cake. Attach the ribs to the fan with dots of icing. Mix gold powder with lemon extract and paint the wheat.

To make the rope border, roll out 2 fondant cords, each long enough to wrap around the cake, and twist them together. Attach the twisted rope to the bottom edge of the cake with a little water. To make the tasseled rope, press fondant through the ¼-inch-circle die of the clay gun and make 2 cords, each 8 inches long. Twist them together and position the rope on the base,

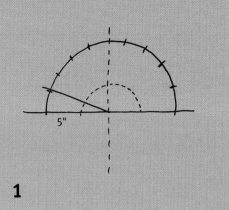

1

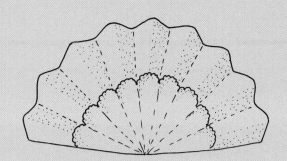

2

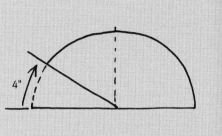

3

6

5

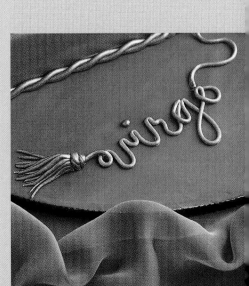

attaching one end to the cake as shown in the photograph on page 33. Shape a long, single cord into the word *Virgo* and attach it to the base as shown. Make the 2 tassels out of many small cords of fondant, pressed through the ⅛-inch-circle die of the clay gun. Gather them into 2 small bundles, pressing the tops together. Attach them as shown in the photograph, covering the seams with small gum-paste cords. To make the medallion (**6**), cut a piece of gum paste with the daisy cutter and emboss it with the umbrella tool, or use my medallion mold (see "Sources"). Attach it with royal icing over the ends of the cords. Mix gold powder with lemon extract and paint the ropes and the medallion.

4

libra
cake

SERVES 45

The sculpted scale decoration is a tipoff that this cake is for anyone whose birthday falls under the sign of Libra. It's also an apt choice for your favorite attorney, since the scales of justice are the symbol of law.

In advance:

Outline the scalloped cake pan on one of the foamcore boards OR enlarge pattern **1** by 176 percent and trace its dotted outline on the board. Cut out the shape with the X-acto knife. To make the base, cut a second board, using the first one as a template and enlarging it 1½ inches on all sides with the roll of masking tape (see the section on cake bases, page 175). Glue the second board to the center of the third, placing something heavy on top to keep it flat while it dries. When the glue is dry, cut the third board to match the second. Cover the base with thinned pale-green royal icing. Let dry. Glue the ribbon around the edge.

To decorate:

Bake the cake and let it cool completely. Fill the layers and assemble them. If you have baked an oval cake, you will now need to carve it into a scalloped shape. Place the board on top of the

- cake:
  13-by-9-inch scalloped oval, 2½ inches high, baked in a scalloped oval pan OR in a 13-by-9⅞-inch oval pan
- 3 14-inch round foamcore boards
- X-acto knife
- 1½-inch-thick roll of masking tape
- white glue
- royal icing (page 147)
- colors:
- moss-green and sky-blue paste
- green and teal airbrush paint

- ½-inch-wide teal ribbon
- serrated knife
- rolled fondant (page 145)
- airbrush
- gum-paste veining tool and umbrella tool

35

cake and, using the serrated knife, cut away the sides of the cake a little at a time to match the shape of the board. Attach the cake to the board.

Crumb-coat the cake (see page 150) and chill it. Cover the cake with sky-blue fondant. Use the airbrush to spray the top green. Attach the cake to the base with a little royal icing.

Following pattern **1**, form the scale from pieces of blue fondant and attach them to the top of the cake with a little water. For each rope, roll out a ¼-inch-thick cord of fondant, 8 inches long. Fold it in half and twist the two halves together. Emboss the curved lines at the top of the scale with the veining tool, and the holes in the band with the umbrella tool.

Using the airbrush, spray teal around the scale and the edges of the cake. Roll a ¼-inch-thick cord of blue fondant and place it around the top edge.

1

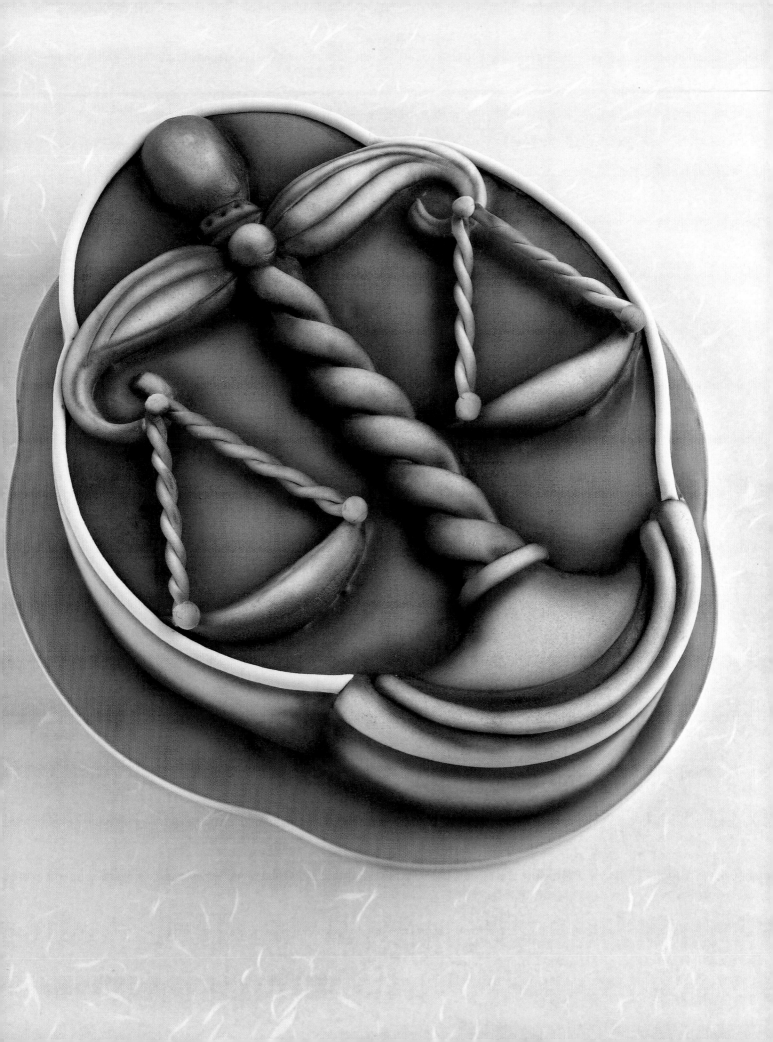

sweet scorpio

SERVES 15–20

For some people, a giant cookie is a birthday wish come true. If you're a Scorpio, the mosaic of candies on top means it's all for you.

To decorate:
Bake the cookie and let it cool completely. Cover the top of the cookie with black royal icing. Let dry.

Enlarge the scorpion pattern (**1**) by 230 percent and cut it out. Place the pattern on the cookie and outline it with piping gel. Using the photograph on page 38 as a guide, fill in the design, and then the background, with candies, brushing each area with piping gel before attaching the candies with the tweezers.

1

- 1 Giant Cookie (page 148), 18 inches round
- 18-inch round base
- royal icing (page 147)
- black paste food coloring
- clear piping gel
- paintbrush
- tweezers
- assorted candies:
– 300 black M&Ms (8.5 ounces)
– 230 blue M&Ms (6.5 ounces)
– 230 dark-blue M&Ms (6.5 ounces)
– 60 brown mini M&Ms (1 ounce)
– 150 blue mini M&Ms (2.5 ounces)
– 800 ¼-inch-wide red mini jawbreakers (13.5 ounces)
– 225 ¼-inch-wide blue mini jawbreakers (3.75 ounces)
– 140 ³⁄₁₆-inch-wide silver dragées
– 80 ⅜-inch-wide silver dragées
– 25 ¼-inch-wide silver dragées

crazy quilt

SERVES 18   A Rosenthal china pattern inspired this tiny cake with its bright-colored fondant cutouts. Because I made it for a Sagittarian's birthday, the playful patchwork incorporates arrow designs to represent the sign of the archer.

- cakes:
  - 2½-inch square, 1¾ inches high
  - 5-inch octagon, 2 inches high
  - 7-inch octagon, 3 inches high
- 2½-inch square, 5-inch round, and 7-inch round foamcore boards
- ruler
- X-acto knife
- 10-inch round base, ½ inch high
- royal icing (page 147)
- colors: moss-green, yellow, royal-blue, red, black, turquoise, pink, rose, orange, kelly-green, willow-green, and purple paste
- ½-inch-wide white ribbon
- white glue
- ⅛-inch-wide yellow ribbon (optional)
- gum paste (page 154)
- gum-paste umbrella tool
- serrated knife
- rolled fondant (page 145)
- pizza cutter or PME cutting wheel
- pastry bags and couplers
- tip: #12

In advance:

Make the patterns for the cakes and boards. To make the octagon for the bottom tier, outline the bottom of the 7-inch round pan on a sheet of paper and cut it out. Fold the paper circle in half, then into quarters, then into eighths. Using a ruler, draw a line across the two points that form the ends of the arc and cut off the rounded part (see the dotted line in figure **1**). Unfold the paper, place it flat on the largest foamcore board, and cut around the outline with the X-acto knife. For the 5-inch tier, follow the same steps to make an octagonal paper pattern, then draw two 1-inch lines in a V shape between each of the points around the octagon (the solid line in figure **1**). Place the pattern on the middle-sized foamcore board and cut out the star shape.

Cover the base with pale-green royal icing and let it dry. Glue the white ribbon around the edge. If you desire, run 2 lengths of yellow ribbon over the white ribbon, gluing the ends together.

Now make the 3 gum-paste arrows (**2**, **3**, and **4**). Tint small pieces of gum paste yellow, blue, green, red, and black. Make the shafts by rolling out 3 3/16-inch-thick cords, each 3 inches long. Use the X-acto knife to cut the feathers and the arrowheads in the colors shown in the photograph on page 40. Emboss the bottom of the blue arrowhead with the umbrella tool. Let the arrow pieces dry overnight, then glue them together with royal icing.

To decorate:

Bake the cakes and let them cool completely. Fill the tiers and assemble them. Place the corresponding boards on top of the same sized cakes and use the serrated knife to carve the tiers to match the shapes of the boards. Crumb-coat the tiers (see page 150) and chill them. Cover the bottom tier with pale-blue fondant, the middle one with yellow fondant, and the top one with pale-green fondant. Stack the tiers on the base so that the points of the octagonal tier line up with the recessed points on the center tier. Attach the tiers to each other and to the base with royal icing.

Use the paste colors to tint small pieces of fondant individually, referring to the photograph on page 43. Roll out the pieces and cut them with the pizza cutter or the cutting wheel, then brush the back of each piece with a little water to attach it to the cake. Cut the circles with the #12 tip.

Roll out a 1/4-inch-thick cord of white fondant, making it long enough to wrap around the base of the bottom tier. Roll out a slightly thinner fondant cord for the center tier and then a third cord, slightly thinner than the last, for the top tier. Cut 1/2-inch squares of black fondant, brush them with a little water, and attach them to the border of the bottom tier, 1/2 inch apart. Repeat on the center tier with 1/4-by-1/2-inch rectangles, and on the top tier with 3/16-inch squares separated by 1/4 inch.

Attach the arrows to the cake with royal icing, as shown in the photograph on page 43.

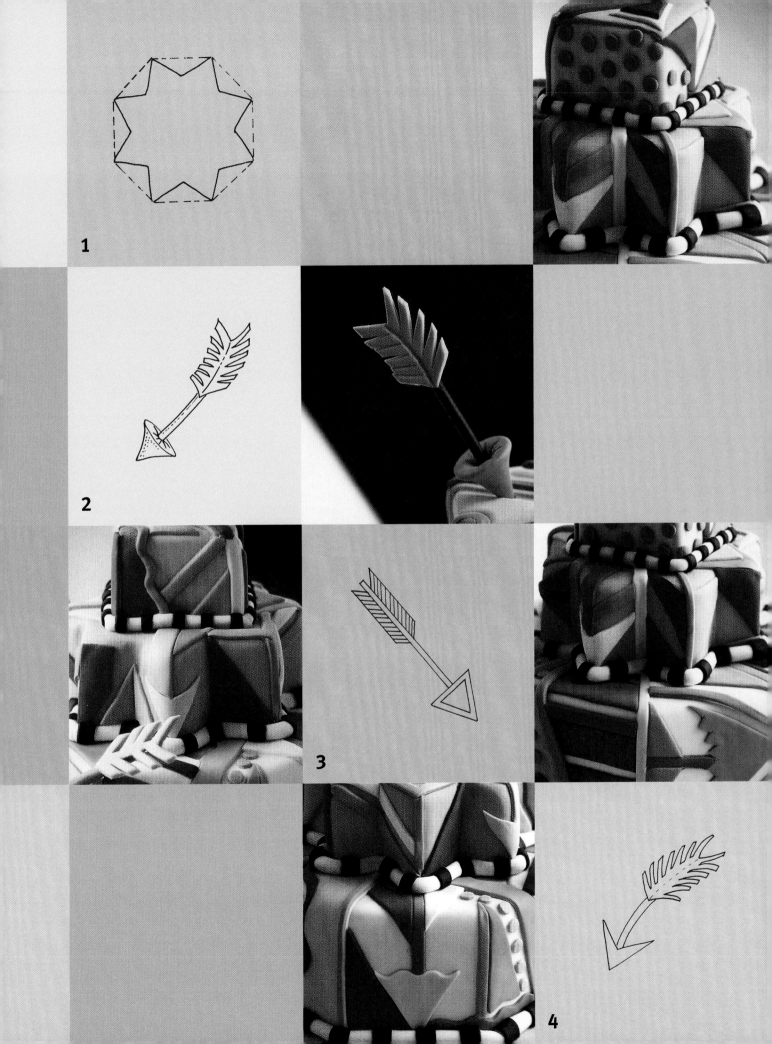

the queen's purse

SERVES 16

Ever wondered what the Queen of England carries in her handbag? All of these would-be royal accessories are edible: the purse is made of cake, and the lipstick, compact, coin purse, and hankie are gum paste. The gold clasp forms the sign for Capricorn.

- cakes:
- – 9-inch square, 2 inches high
- – 8-inch square, 2 inches high
- compass
- 3 foamcore boards, 2 7 by 4 inches and 1 9 by 4½ inches, plus additional foamcore
- ruler
- triangle
- X-acto knife
- white glue
- masking tape
- rolled fondant (page 145)
- colors:
- – leaf-green, aster-mauve, and lemon-yellow paste
- – nontoxic gold, pink, super pearl, and green iridescent powders
- serrated tracing wheel
- gum paste (page 154)
- wavy-edged pastry wheel

- 3½-, 3-, 2¾-, and 2¼-inch plain round and sunflower fret cutters
- clay gun
- gum-paste veining tool
- plastic cobblestone impression mat
- jar lid 3 inches in diameter
- cornstarch
- pizza cutter
- embossed rolling pin
- lemon extract
- paintbrushes
- royal icing (page 147)
- pastry bags and couplers
- tip: PME #2
- small serrated knife
- ¼-inch-thick wooden dowels

In advance:

To make the support for the purse handle, use the compass to draw a 3¾-inch circle on the extra piece of foamcore. With the ruler, draw a line across the circle and through the midpoint, then lay the triangle along that diameter and use it as one of the shorter sides of a rectangle whose longer sides measure 4⅛ inches (**1**). The rectangle with the half-circle at one end will form the shape of the purse's handle. Cut out the pattern with the X-acto knife. Cut a foamcore strip 15 inches long by 1¼ inches wide and score it halfway through, crosswise, at ⅜-inch intervals (**2**). Keeping the cut side out, bend the strip around the curved foamcore pattern and glue them together, holding them in place while the glue dries with masking tape (**3**).

Tint some fondant lime green (made with lemon-yellow and leaf-green), then roll it out ⅛ inch thick and cut a 15-by-2½-inch strip. Brush

45

one side with a little water and fold it in half lengthwise, with the moist side in. Use the tracing wheel to emboss a line of stitching about $^3/_{16}$ inch from each edge (**4**). Fit the strip over the foamcore handle support, moisten the ends, and fold them back 1 inch. Let the handle dry, standing upright, for 1 day, then remove it from the support and let it dry on its side (**5**).

To make the gum-paste decorations:
To make the compact, roll out a piece of gum paste $^1/_4$ inch thick and cut a circle with the 3-inch plain cutter to form the bottom part. Press enough softened fondant through the half-circle die of the clay gun to make a 10-inch-long cord. Brush the edge of the gum-paste circle with a little water and attach the cord (**6**). Let dry. To make the powder puff and the lid, roll out another piece of gum paste $^1/_8$ inch thick. Cut a circle with the $2^3/_4$-inch plain cutter. Gently press the dull edge of the $2^1/_4$-inch cutter into the gum paste to indent a circle. Let dry. Place the remaining gum paste on the cobblestone impression mat and press it with your fingers. Cut a circle with the $3^1/_2$-inch plain cutter and drape it over the jar lid after dusting it with cornstarch to prevent sticking. Let dry (**7**). Form a $^1/_4$-inch square of gum paste, round the corners, and attach it to the side of the lid for the clasp. Paint the lid and the edge of the bottom with gold powder mixed with lemon extract. Paint the "powder" on the bottom with pink iridescent powder mixed with lemon extract.

To make the lipstick, tint some gum paste mauve and roll it into a $^1/_2$-inch-thick cord 3 inches long. Use a knife to cut one end diagonally, gently softening the cut edge with your fingers to give it the rounded look of a new lipstick. Let dry. To make the tube, roll out another piece of gum paste $^1/_8$ inch thick and cut a

$2^1/_4$-by-2-inch strip with the pizza cutter. Brush one side with water and wrap it around the lipstick so that the 2-inch-long edges meet and the bottom edge lines up with the bottom of the lipstick. Roll out another piece of gum paste $^1/_8$ inch thick. Roll the embossed rolling pin over the surface and cut a $2^1/_4$-by-1-inch strip. Brush the plain side with water and wrap it around the lower part of the lipstick, lining up the edges (**8**). Pinch the seam together. Let dry. Press a small piece of gum paste or fondant through the $^1/_8$-inch-circle die of the clay gun. Cut a $2^1/_4$-inch piece, brush it with water, and attach it to the top edge of the last gum-paste strip.

For the cover of the lipstick tube, roll out a piece of gum paste $^1/_4$ inch thick. Roll the embossed rolling pin over the surface and cut a $2^1/_4$-by-$1^1/_2$-inch strip, one of whose long sides forms a slightly convex curve (**9**). Brush the edge of one of the shorter sides with water, then, keeping the embossed side out, carefully join the edges to form a tube with one angled end. Pinch the seam together and let the tube dry upright. When it is dry, cut an oval of gum paste to fit inside the angled end. Brush its edge with water and carefully attach it to the tube (**10**). Let dry. Mix gold powder with lemon extract and paint the lipstick tube and the cover gold.

To make the coin purse, roll out enough fondant or gum paste to make a 6-inch square $^1/_4$ inch thick. Cut out the square. Brush 2 opposite edges with water and fold them over about $^1/_4$ inch, then place crumpled tissues or paper towels in the center (**11**). Starting with one of the sides that are not folded, pinch the edge together at intervals to create a gathered look (**12**). Flatten the edge with your fingertips and trim it with the pizza cutter. Repeat the process on the opposite edge (**13**), then pull one edge over the tissues and align it with the

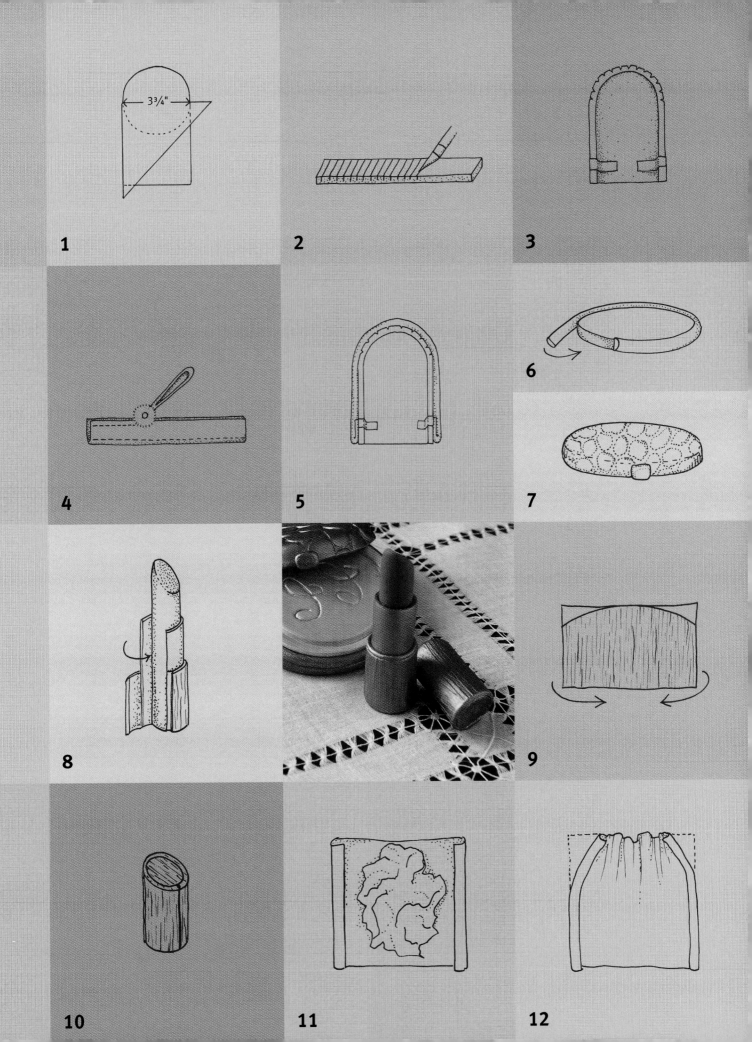

1

2

3

4

5

6

7

8

9

10

11

12

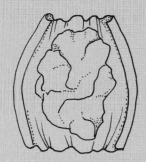

13

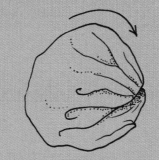

14

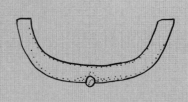

15

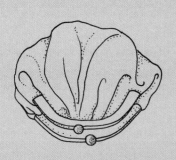

16

17

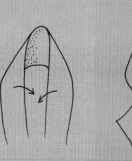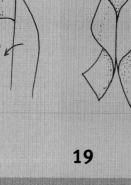

18   **19**   **20**   **21**   **22**   **23**

26

other (**14**). Be sure there are enough tissues inside to make the purse look full. Let dry.

To make the coin purse's metal frame, roll out a piece of gum paste ¼ inch thick and cut two 4½-by-¼-inch strips. Soften the edges with your fingers, then bend the strips into the shape of the frame (**15**; make 2). Let dry. Piping the top edge of the purse with a little royal icing, attach the frame pieces over the gathered edges as shown in figure **16**. Let dry. For the snaps, roll 2 small pieces of gum paste into ½-inch-long teardrops and glue them to the center of the frame pieces with royal icing. Let dry.

Mix pink and white iridescent powder with lemon extract and paint the purse. Mix gold powder with lemon extract and paint the frame.

To make the hankie, roll out a 9-by-7-inch piece of gum paste ⅛ inch thick. Using the wavy-edged pastry wheel, cut a 9-by-7-inch rectangle. Use the fret cutter to cut out teardrop shapes ½ inch apart and ⅛ inch in from the edge (**17**). Cut out a clover shape in each corner. Fold the hankie in half so that it gathers in the center, as shown in the photograph on page 48. Let dry on crumpled paper towels.

To make the fabric flowers, cut a strip of gum paste ¼ inch wide and 4 inches long. Holding the strip horizontally, bring in the 2 ends, folding them over, as shown in **18**. Then fold the strips back again (**19**). Press the 2 ends together to reduce the size of the opening in the top (**20**). Then pinch together the 2 ends to gather the "bud" (**21**). Wrap a second strip around the first "bud" (**22**). Mix pink iridescent powder with lemon extract and paint the buds pale pink. Mix green iridescent powder with lemon extract and paint the leaves pale green. Glue them, in bunches of 3, 1 inch in from the corners of the hankie, using royal icing. With the #2 tip, pipe pointed royal-icing dots above and below the cutouts and on the flowers, as shown in the photograph on page 48. Mix white iridescent powder with lemon extract and paint the dots.

To make the purse's Capricorn clasp (**23**), roll a small piece of gum paste into the indicated shape with your hands.

To decorate:

Bake the cakes and let them cool completely. Cut the cake layers according to the measurements given in figure **24**. (The finished cake will be 7 by 4 inches at the base, 9 by 4½ inches at its widest part, and 5 by 2 inches at the top.) Fill and assemble the 9-inch layers on the 9-by-4½-inch board, then center one of the 7-by-4-inch boards on top. Using the serrated knife, shave off the sides of the cake a little at a time to carve a wedge from the edge of the board to the bottom edge of the tier. Invert the tier so the bigger board is on top, and continue filling and stacking the layers until the cake is 4½ inches high. Insert the dowels (see "Building a Tiered Cake," page 150) and add a layer of lime-green fondant. Center the third board on top and finish filling and stacking the layers.

Starting at the top edge of the 9-inch tier and then moving on to the upper tiers, carefully shave off the cake a little at a time with the serrated knife to carve out the shape of the purse (**24** and **25**). Crumb-coat the cake (see page 150) and chill it. Cover the entire cake with lime-green fondant. Use the tracing wheel to emboss a double row of stitching along the front and back edges and over the top of the cake. Roll out a ¼-inch-thick cord of fondant long enough to wrap around the base.

Cut out the flap, the front straps, and the side loops with metal rings. With the tracing wheel, emboss stitching ³⁄₁₆ inch in from the edge of each piece. Brush the back of the flap with a little water and drape it over the top of the cake and 2 inches down the back. Attach the straps to the front of the purse as shown in figure **24**. Fasten. Attach the side loops to the cake so the folded edge is flush with the top of the flap (**26**).

Place the handle on the cake. Attach the ends of the metal rings to the front and back of the bottom of the handle. Attach the Capricorn clasp to the front of the cake. Mix gold powder with lemon extract and paint the clasp and rings.

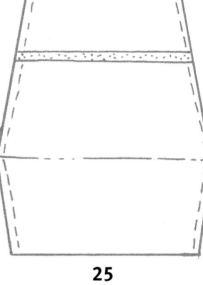

25

24

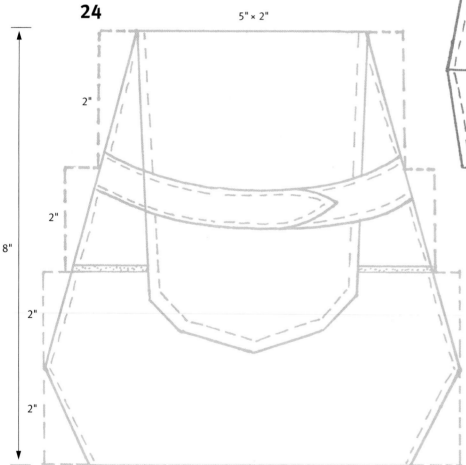

5" × 2"

2"

2"

8"

2"

2"

2"

flowers

of

the month

little flower cakes

SERVES 1 Each of these twelve cakes displays the flower of one month of the year (all are listed on pages 54 and 57). What a sweet birthday surprise: a personal cake decorated with your special flower.

In advance:

Make the gum-paste flowers and leaves for your desired month's cake. Cover the base with foil wrap.

To decorate:

To bake a quantity of these cakes, you can bake a shallow ½-sheet pan of batter and then cut the cakes with a 2½-inch cutter. Or you can bake them in cupcake tins. Bake the cake and let it cool completely. Fill the layers and assemble them on the base. Crumb-coat the cake (see page 150) and chill it. Tint the fondant as directed below and roll it out ¼-inch thick. Cut out a 6-inch circle and drape it evenly over the cake, smoothing only the top. The fondant will naturally fall into folds, which you can accentuate or rearrange as you wish. Decorate the cake as directed below. Attach the gum-paste flowers and leaves to the top of the cake.

- cake:
  2½-inch round,
  2½ inches high
- gum-paste flowers and leaves (page 156)
- 4½-inch round foamcore base, ³⁄₁₆ inch high
- silver or gold food-grade foil wrap
- rolled fondant (page 145)
- colors:
  see directions for individual cakes
- cutters and tools:
  see directions for individual cakes
- pastry bags and couplers
- tips:
  see directions for individual cakes
- royal icing (page 147)
- paintbrushes

SNOWDROP (JANUARY)

Knead buttercup, caramel, and paprika paste colorings into white fondant to tint it a light butterscotch color. Cover the cake.

Decorations: Roll out a thin piece of white fondant. Cut out 10 to 12 circles with a ½-inch round cutter. Cut 2 deep notches on one edge of each circle. Attach the circles to the cake with royal icing. Pipe light-green royal-icing stems and leaves with the PME #2 tip (**1**).

VIOLET (FEBRUARY)

Knead violet and mulberry paste colorings into white fondant. Cover the cake.

Decorations: Roll out a thin piece of fondant the same color as the cake. Cut out 10 to 12 flowers with a Wilton forget-me-not cutter. Thin the petals with a gum-paste ball tool and press the ball tool into the center of each flower to cup them. Attach the flowers to the cake with royal icing and pipe a dot of white icing in the center of each one (**2**).

JONQUIL (MARCH)

Knead bitter-lemon and eggshell paste coloring into white fondant. Cover the cake.

Decorations: Cut out 7 flowers in white fondant with a 1-inch daisy cutter. Attach them to the cake with royal icing. Using a PME #2 tip, pipe a dot of yellow royal icing in the center of each flower and a circle of white royal icing around the dot. Overpipe 2 circles of white icing on each flower, ending with a circle of yellow (**3**). Attach the flowers to the cake with royal icing.

DAISY (APRIL)

Knead melon paste coloring into white fondant. Cover the cake.

Decorations: Roll out a thin piece of white fondant. Cut out 7 or 8 flowers with a Wilton for-get-me-not cutter. Attach them to the cake with royal icing. Pipe small yellow dots in the center of each one (**4**).

LILY OF THE VALLEY (MAY)

Knead willow- and moss-green paste colors into white fondant. Cover the cake.

Decorations: Roll out a very thin piece of white fondant. Cut out 20 to 25 flowers with the smallest Wilton forget-me-not cutter. Use the gum-paste ball tool to cup the petals. Attach the flowers to the cake in clusters of 2 or 3, using royal icing. With a PME #2 tip, pipe a dot of green icing in the center of each flower (**5**). Pipe a green line for the stem, then add a few white dots on each cluster for the buds.

ROSE (JUNE)

Knead caramel paste coloring into white fondant to tint it antique white. Cover the cake.

Decorations: Roll out a thin piece of white fondant. Cut out 7 or 8 circles with a ¾-inch round cutter. Attach the circles to the cake with royal icing. Using a PME #2 tip, pipe royal icing in a spiral out from the center (**6**).

WATER LILY (JULY)

Knead Miami mauve paste coloring into white fondant. Cover the cake.

Decorations: Roll out 2 thin pieces of fondant, one pink and the other pale yellow. Cut out 8 or 9 pink flowers with a Wilton small daisy cutter. Cut out 8 or 9 yellow flowers with a Wilton forget-me-not cutter, and the same number with a Wilton baby's-breath cutter. Attach the larger yellow flower to the cake with royal icing. Then attach the pink one to the center of the yellow one with royal icing. Then attach the smaller yellow flower to the center. Pipe a dot of pale-blue royal icing in the center of each (**7**).

1

Snowdrop

2

Violet

3

Jonquil

4

Daisy

5

Lily of the Valley

6

Rose

7

Water Lily

8

Poppy

9

Morning Glory

10

Marigold

11

Chrysanthemum

12

Narcissus and Holly

POPPY (AUGUST)

Knead Georgia peach paste coloring into white fondant to give it a pale-peach tint. Cover the cake.

Decorations: Roll out a thin piece of deep-pink fondant. Cut out 8 to 9 flowers with a small 6-petaled cutter. Use a gum-paste ball tool to thin and cup the petals. Pipe black dots in the center of each flower with royal icing (**8**). Attach the flowers to the cake with royal icing.

MORNING GLORY (SEPTEMBER)

Knead delphinium- and cornflower-blue paste colorings into white fondant. Cover the cake.

Decorations: Roll out a thin piece of fondant the same color as the cake. Cut out 8 or 9 circles with a ½-inch round cutter. Attach the flowers to the cake with royal icing. Using the #2 tip, pipe a small dot of white royal icing in the center of each circle, then drag the tip to the edge. Repeat 5 times. Pipe a yellow dot in the center of each flower (**9**).

MARIGOLD (OCTOBER)

Work a small amount of pink, yellow, and turquoise paste colorings into white fondant and knead enough to marbleize. Cover the cake.

Decorations: Roll out a thin piece of pale-yellow fondant. Cut out 10 to 12 flowers each with Wilton forget-me-not and baby's-breath cutters. Attach the flowers to the cake with royal icing. Attach the smaller flowers to the larger ones with royal icing. Using a small paintbrush, paint a small amount of brownish-red liquid color in the center of each flower. Pipe a small dot of pale-blue royal icing in the center (**10**).

CHRYSANTHEMUM (NOVEMBER)

Knead Christmas red paste coloring into white fondant to tint it dark pink. Cover the cake.

Decorations: Roll out a thin piece of fondant the same color as the cake. Cut out 8 or 9 flowers with a Wilton small daisy cutter (**11**). Attach them to the cake with royal icing.

NARCISSUS AND HOLLY (DECEMBER)

Knead forest-green and royal-blue paste colorings into white fondant to tint it turquoise. Cover the cake.

Decorations: Roll out a thin piece of white fondant. Cut out 4 or 5 flowers with a Wilton small daisy cutter. Attach them to the cake with royal icing. Using a #2 tip, pipe a circle of yellow royal icing in the center of each flower. Overpipe 2 more circles. Roll out a piece of green fondant and cut out 4 to 5 leaves with a holly-leaf cutter. Attach the leaves to the cake with royal icing. For the holly berries, pipe red dots with the #2 tip (**12**).

please
eat the
daisies

SERVES 20 To celebrate an April birthday, I designed a heart-shaped royal-icing collar (a delicate border made separately that extends over the top edge of the cake), inspired by British designs. The daisy, this month's flower, is surrounded by sweet peas, lilacs, and fragile tendrils.

1

- cake:
  9¼-inch heart,
  3 inches high
- 10-inch-square foamcore board
- 2 14-inch round foamcore boards for base
- X-acto knife
- 1¼-inch-thick roll of masking tape
- white glue
- wax paper or silicone-coated parchment paper
- pastry bags and couplers
- tips: PME #2, PME #3, #233

- colors:
- moss-green, white, rose-petal, violet, sky-blue, yellow, and leaf-green paste
- nontoxic moss-green, rose, and lime-green powder
- royal icing (page 147)
- small paintbrushes
- clear piping gel
- rolled fondant (page 145)
- ½-inch-wide blue ribbon
- palette knife

In advance:

Enlarge pattern **1** by 155 percent, trace it on the 10-inch board, and cut out the shape with the X-acto knife. To make the base, cut one of the 14-inch boards, using the 10-inch board as a template and enlarging it 1¼ inches on all sides with the roll of masking tape (see page 175). Glue the cut board to the remaining board. When the glue is dry, cut around the heart-shaped board with the X-acto knife.

To make the royal-icing collar, enlarge pattern **2**, place it on a cookie sheet, and tape a sheet of wax or parchment paper on top. You will be using the run-in-sugar technique (see page 170) with overpiping (see page 152) and brush embroidery (see page 172). You will also need to make a few extra daisies from the pattern to place around the sides of the cake (**3**).

Using the #3 tip, pipe the vines with moss-green royal icing, then overpipe with the #2 tip. Outline the leaves in the same color and fill them in with thinned icing. Let dry. Outline and fill in the daisies with white icing and the sweet peas with pink icing, letting each color dry before adding the next. Make the extra daisies. Pipe purple dots for the lilacs. Let all dry overnight.

When the collar is completely dry, finish the leaves and flowers with brush embroidery. Brush the larger leaves with pale-green icing, using short, diagonal strokes moving toward the center to resemble veining. Brush moss-green icing down the length of the tiny leaves. For the daisies, pipe white icing on the ends of each petal and brush toward the center, using long strokes. Brush the sweet peas with pale-pink icing, using short strokes going from the edge toward the center, overlapping the blossoms. Pipe yellow icing in the center of the daisies with the #233 tip. With the #2 tip, pipe a thin line of pale-green icing down the center of the leaves.

Mix the powdered colors with a little water to paint the highlights and shading, so the colors will blend with those of the previous layer. Paint the leaves moss green, leaving the edges pale green. Paint the center of the sweet-pea petals rose. Paint lime green around the center of the daisies and on some of the petals.

To decorate:
Bake the cake and let it cool completely. Fill the layers and assemble them on the board. Crumb-coat the cake (see page 150) and chill it. Attach the cake to the base with royal icing. Spread a thin layer of piping gel on the base around the cake so the fondant will adhere to it easily. Make sure that you roll out enough sky-blue fondant to cover both the cake and the

base with one piece. Trim the fondant at the top edge of the base and glue the ribbon around the edge.

Slide a thin palette knife under the run-in sugar design and carefully remove it from the paper; it is very delicate and breakable. Place it on the cake, attaching it with a little royal icing. Attach the extra daisies at an angle to the side and the base, using dots of royal icing.

2 enlarge 230%

3 enlarge 168%

damask rose cake

SERVES 12

This miniature tiered cake, perfect for an intimate gathering, displays a lush floral design made with brush embroidery. Although the rose is traditionally June's flower, this pretty cake is a dessert for all seasons.

1

To decorate:

Bake the cakes and let them cool. Fill the tiers and assemble them on their corresponding boards. Crumb-coat the tiers (see page 150) and chill them. Cover the tiers with ivory fondant. Insert dowels in the bottom tier, and stack the tiers, using the decorative plate as a base, if desired.

Enlarge pattern **1** by 135 percent and trace it on a sheet of paper. Place the pattern against the cake and outline it by pricking holes in it with the long pin. Using white royal icing, brush-embroider the design (see page 172). Let dry. Paint the leaves, starting with leaf green and adding highlights of moss green. Next, paint the 2 uppermost flowers with highlights of pink and pink mixed with purple. Paint the largest flower with lemon yellow and the 2 bottom flowers pink mixed with purple.

Pipe a snail trail (see page 152) of royal icing around each tier and the base, using the #3 tip on the top tier, the #6 tip on the middle one, and the #9 tip around the bottom and the base. Mix gold powder with lemon extract and paint the center of the largest flower and all of the borders.

- cakes:
  - 2-inch round, 2½ inches high
  - 4-inch round, 1½ inches high
  - 5-inch round, 3 inches high
- 2-, 4-, and 5-inch-round foamcore boards
- ivory rolled fondant (page 145)
- ¼-inch-thick wooden dowels
- 8-inch decorative plate (optional)

- long pin
- royal icing (page 147)
- small paintbrush
- colors:
  - nontoxic leaf-green, moss-green, pink, purple, and lemon-yellow petal dust
  - gold iridescent powder
- pastry bags and couplers
- tips: PME #3, #6, #9
- lemon extract

63

french flower garden

SERVES 50   A nineteenth-century wedding-cake decoration inspired this beautiful cake overflowing with blossoms. The flowers included here represent every month of the year.

- cake
  - 12-inch petal, 4 inches high
- gum-paste flowers and leaves (see pages 53–57 for specific ingredients/ materials and instructions):
  - 100 snowdrops on stems
  - 15 violets
  - 10 jonquils, 7 of them with stems
  - 15 daisies, 13 of them with stems
  - 10 lilies of the valley
  - 15 small and 5 large roses
  - 10 water lilies, 4 of them with stems
  - 6 poppies, 3 of them with stems
  - 10 morning glories
  - 15 sweet peas
  - 15 marigolds and 5 marigold buds
  - 15 chrysanthemums, 10 of them with stems
  - 10 narcissi
  - 30 holly sprigs
  - 100 assorted leaves, 65 of them on stems
- florist's tape
- 12-, 14-, and 15-inch round foamcore boards, ¼ inch thick

- X-acto knife
- 1-inch-thick roll of masking tape
- 15-inch petal cake pan
- white glue
- royal icing (page 147)
- colors:
  - lemon-yellow and green paste
  - nontoxic white iridescent powder
- pastry bags and couplers
- tips: PME #3, #8, #18
- ¼-inch-wide white ribbon
- 4-inch Styrofoam ball
- 5-inch cherub sculpture or other decorative support
- hot-glue gun
- rolled fondant (page 145)
- large S-shaped crimper
- lemon extract
- paintbrush
- ¼-inch-thick wooden dowels

In advance:

Make all of the gum-paste flowers and leaves according to the instructions provided on pages 53–57. Let dry. To form the 2 trailing vines, use florist's tape to fasten some stemmed leaves and flowers together — enough to measure about 8 inches long (**1**).

Outline the 12-inch petal cake pan on the smallest board and cut out the shape with the X-acto knife. To make the stepped cake base, cut the 14-inch board, using the 12-inch petal pan as a template and enlarging it with the roll of masking tape (see page 150). Outline a 15-inch petal cake pan on the third board and cut it out. Glue the 2 larger boards together, with the biggest one extending out ½ inch on all sides, and let them dry. Place something heavy on top to hold the boards flat while the glue dries.

Cover the base with thinned lemon-yellow royal icing. Let dry. Using the #3 tip, pipe a dot border (see page 152) of lemon-yellow royal icing along the edge of the smaller board. Glue the ribbon around the outer edge of the largest board.

Attach the Styrofoam ball to the top of the cherub with hot glue. Starting at the top and working down, insert stemmed flowers and leaves into the Styrofoam. With the #18 tip, pipe green royal icing around the stems as you work, to cover the Styrofoam.

To decorate:

Bake the cake and let it cool completely. Fill the layers and assemble them on the board. Crumb-coat the cake (see page 150) and chill it. Cover the cake with lemon-yellow fondant.

With the crimper, emboss a continuous S-shaped border along the top edge and vertical lines 1 inch apart down the side of the cake. Attach it to the base with royal icing. Mix white iridescent powder with lemon extract and paint the sections between the crimping, leaving every fourth section unpainted. Using the #8 tip, pipe a dot border of lemon-yellow royal icing along the bottom edge of the cake. Insert dowels to support the base of the statue.

Place the cherub and his Styrofoam bouquet on the center of the cake, attaching it with royal icing. Insert the remaining stemmed flowers and leaves in the top and edges of the cake. Add the trailing vines to both sides of the bouquet. Attach the unstemmed flowers and leaves around the top of the cake, using royal icing.

1

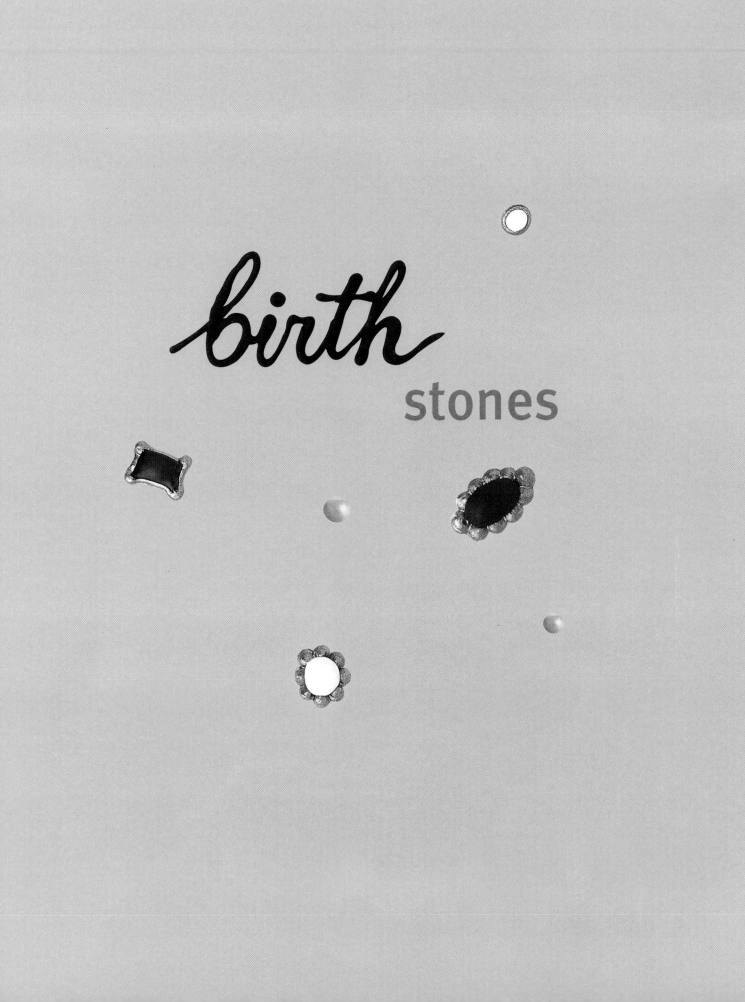

birth stones

les bijoux des mois

SERVES 1

This collection of bejeweled, edible trinkets, inspired by decorative doorknobs, showcases ten of the year's twelve birthstones. The decorations may look like perfume bottles of Tiffany glass, but they're actually made of chocolate. Because tempering chocolate can be tricky, I've used confectionery coating, which has a sweeter flavor and is very easy to work with.

In advance:

To make the confectionery-coating molds in the desired colors, melt the coating as directed on the package. Pour the melted coating into the molds and chill until firm. You can make the larger molds hollow by pouring in the coating and then pouring off the excess so that only the sides are coated. Repeat the process if necessary to thicken the sides. Mix the iridescent powdered colors with lemon extract and paint the sections as shown in the accompanying photographs.

Make the modeling chocolate for the hand-formed decorations in the desired colors. For ivory, mix a little brown with white confectionery coating. For flesh, mix pink and butterscotch confectionery coating. Wrap the colors separately in

- confectionery coating
- modeling chocolate (page 144)
- various molds and tools *(see individual ingredients/materials lists below for equipment needed)*
- nontoxic iridescent powdered colors *(see individual ingredients lists below for colors needed)*
- lemon extract
- small paintbrushes
- pastry bag and couplers
- tip: PME #2
- royal icing (page 147)
- colored piping gel or clear piping gel, mixed with liquid food coloring

JANUARY
(GARNET)

- 1½-inch square fluted tart pan, ½ inch high
- 1½-inch square plain tart pan, ½ inch high
- 3¼-inch-wide oval fluted tart pan with a 2-inch-wide bottom, 1 inch high
- pale-violet, pale-blue, and blue confectionery coating
- pale-pink, green, and yellow modeling chocolate

- nontoxic gold, pale-pink, green, yellow, pale-blue, and cobalt-blue iridescent powdered colors, mixed with lemon extract
- red piping gel
-
- 2-inch round fluted tart pan, ¾ inch high
- 2½-inch round fluted tart pan, ¾ inch high
- 3½-inch-wide cup with a 2-inch-wide bottom, 2½ inches high
- 1½-inch round plain tart pan, ¾ inch high
- PME gum-paste shell tool
- blue and yellow confectionery coating
- pale-blue, pale-green, green, and pink modeling chocolate
- nontoxic violet, cobalt-blue, yellow, pink, green, blue, and gold iridescent powdered colors, mixed with lemon extract
- orange piping gel

(continued)

FEBRUARY
(AMETHYST)

- 2 1½-inch square plain tart pans, ½ inch high
- 2 3-inch-wide oval fluted tart pans, 1 inch high
- green, blue, and orange confectionery coating
- yellow, pale-blue, and ivory modeling chocolate
- nontoxic gold, yellow, blue, green, and orange iridescent powdered colors, mixed with lemon extract
- violet piping gel

●

- 1½-inch-wide triangular tart pan, ½ inch high
- 1½-inch round plain tart pan, ¾ inch high
- 2½-inch round fluted tart pan, 1 inch high
- blue, orange, and yellow confectionery coating
- pale-blue and pale-green modeling chocolate
- nontoxic pale-blue, cobalt-blue, flesh, yellow, and gold iridescent powdered colors, mixed with lemon extract
- violet piping gel

MARCH
(AQUAMARINE)

- 1½-inch round plain tart pan, ¾ inch high
- 2½-inch round plain tart pan, with a 1½-inch-wide bottom, 1 inch high
- 3-inch-wide half-ball mold
- pale-blue, blue, and red confectionery coating

- pale-pink, white, pale-green, and ivory modeling chocolate
- nontoxic gold, pale-pink, and cobalt-blue iridescent powdered colors, mixed with lemon extract
- sky-blue piping gel

MAY
(EMERALD)

- 1½-inch round plain tart pan, ¾ inch high
- 2 round fluted tart pans, one ¾ inch high and the other 1 inch high
- pale-pink, pale-green, and blue confectionery coating
- pale-green and blue modeling chocolate
- nontoxic gold, pale-green, and pale-pink iridescent powdered colors, mixed with lemon extract
- green piping gel

●

- 2-inch-wide round mold, 1 inch high
- 2 2¾-inch round fluted tart pans, one ¾ inch high and the other 1 inch high
- 1½-inch-wide round plain tart pan, ¾ inch high
- pale-blue, green, blue, and red confectionery coating
- pale-blue, flesh, and pale-pink modeling chocolate
- nontoxic pale-blue, pale-pink, green, and gold iridescent powdered colors, mixed with lemon extract
- dark-green piping gel

plastic wrap and let them set for a few hours or overnight.

To make the ropes, roll cords of modeling chocolate long enough to wrap around the molds. The thinner ropes should be ⅛ inch thick, and the thicker ones ¼ inch thick. Twist them together and attach them to the bijoux. The modeling chocolate should be sticky enough to adhere, but if not, brush it with a little water. With your hands, shape small pieces of modeling chocolate into balls, teardrops, rounded disks, or other decorations.

To decorate:

Assemble the bijoux as shown in the photographs, gluing them together with royal icing. Using the #2 tip, pipe the royal-icing decorations. Mix gold powder with lemon extract and paint the piped decorations. Pipe the gemstones with colored piping gel.

JULY
(RUBY)

- 2 2-inch round fluted tart pans, ¾ inch high
- 3½-inch-wide half-ball mold, 1½ inches high
- 3½-inch round fluted tart pan, 1½ inches high
- 2-inch-wide round tart pan, ½ inch high
- yellow, blue, lemon-yellow, red, and pale-blue confectionery coating
- pale-green and pale-blue modeling chocolate
- nontoxic gold, pale-green, yellow, pale-blue, and lemon-yellow iridescent powdered colors, mixed with lemon extract
- red piping gel

●

- 2 1½-inch square fluted tart pans, ½ inch high
- 2 3½-inch-wide half-ball molds
- 1 2¾-inch round fluted tart pan, ¾ inch high
- light-blue, ivory, butterscotch, and red confectionery coating
- pale-green, pale-blue, and pink modeling chocolate
- nontoxic gold, pale-green, pale-blue, and pale-yellow iridescent powdered colors, mixed with lemon extract
- red piping gel

(continued)

AUGUST
(PERIDOT)

- 7/8-inch-wide round cutter
- 1½-inch square plain tart pan, ½ inch high
- 1½-inch square fluted tart pan, ½ inch high
- orange and blue confectionery coating
- pale-green, pale-pink, and green modeling chocolate
- nontoxic gold, pale-green, and orange iridescent powdered colors, mixed with lemon extract
- green piping gel

●

- 2 2½-inch round fluted tart pans, 1 inch high
- 2 1½-inch square fluted flat-bottomed tart pans, ½ inch high
- blue, pale-blue, and butterscotch confectionery coating
- pale-blue, orange, and lemon-yellow modeling chocolate
- nontoxic pale-blue, orange, lemon-yellow, cobalt-blue, and gold iridescent powdered colors, mixed with lemon extract
- pale-green piping gel

SEPTEMBER
(SAPPHIRE)

- 2 3½-inch-wide half-ball molds
- pale-blue and blue confectionery coating
- flesh, pale-blue, and pale-pink modeling chocolate

- nontoxic gold, violet, pale-pink, pale-blue, and cobalt-blue iridescent powdered colors, mixed with lemon extract
- blue piping gel

OCTOBER
(OPAL)

- 2 2-inch round fluted tart pans, ½ inch high
- 7/8-inch-wide round cutter
- 2¾-inch round fluted tart pan, 1½ inches high
- 3½-inch-wide half-ball mold, 1½ inches high
- PME gum-paste shell tool
- pale-blue, orange, and pale-green confectionery coating
- lemon-yellow, pale-green, and pale-pink modeling chocolate
- nontoxic lemon-yellow, orange, pale-pink, pale-green, and gold iridescent powdered colors, mixed with lemon extract
- white iridescent powdered color, mixed with clear, pink, green, and blue piping gel

●

- 2 1¾-inch round fluted tart pans, ½ inch high
- 3½-inch-wide half-ball mold, 1½ inches high
- 3½-inch round fluted tart pan with a 2-inch-wide bottom, 1½ inches high
- PME gum-paste shell tool
- pale-green, ivory, pale-pink, and butterscotch

---

confectionery coating
- butterscotch and pale-green modeling chocolate
- nontoxic gold, pale-green, and pale-pink iridescent powdered colors, mixed with lemon extract
- white iridescent powdered color, mixed with clear, pink, green, and blue piping gel

NOVEMBER
(TOPAZ)

- 2-inch round mold, 1 inch high
- 2½-inch round fluted tart pan, ¾ inch high
- 2 3¾-inch-wide round fluted tart pans, 1¼ inches high
- PME gum-paste shell tool
- orange, butterscotch, yellow, and pale-blue confectionery coating
- pale-pink and yellow modeling chocolate
- nontoxic pale-pink, orange, yellow, and gold iridescent powdered colors, mixed with lemon extract
- orange piping gel

●

- 2 2-inch round fluted tart pans, ¾ inch high
- 3-inch round fluted tart pan with a 2-inch-wide bottom, ¾ inch high
- 3½-inch-wide cup with a 2-inch-wide bottom, 2½ inches high
- pale-blue, pink, yellow,

---

and orange confectionery coating
- pale-green and yellow modeling chocolate
- nontoxic pale-green, pale-blue, yellow, orange, and gold iridescent powdered colors, mixed with lemon extract
- orange piping gel

DECEMBER
(TURQUOISE)

- 1½-inch round plain tart pan, ¾ inch high
- 3½-inch-wide cup with a 2-inch-wide bottom, 2½ inches high
- pale-blue confectionery coating
- ivory, green, and pale-green modeling chocolate
- nontoxic pale-green, white, pale-blue, and gold iridescent powdered colors, mixed with lemon extract
- sky-blue royal icing, for piping the gems

crown
of pearls

This elegant little cake celebrates June birthdays with an abundance of that month's gems. The pearls may be gum paste, but when they are so lovingly made, who needs the real thing?

In advance:

Roll pieces of gum paste into balls of various sizes, from ¼ inch to 1 inch in diameter. To decorate the cake tiers, you will need 64 ¼-inch, 56 5/16-inch, 74 ⅜-inch, 32 ½-inch, and 9 ¾-inch pearls. Make 150 more, in an assortment of sizes from ¼ inch to 1 inch, to arrange around the base. Set the soft gum-paste balls on the foam pad to keep them round while they dry. When the pearls are dry, mix super pearl iridescent powder with lemon extract and paint them.

Using the pliers, bend the wire to form the word *June,* leaving enough wire at one end to insert into the cake. With the #2 tip, pipe dots of royal icing on the wire. Let dry. Mix super pearl iridescent powder with lemon extract and paint the dots.

To decorate:

Bake the cakes and let them cool completely. Fill the tiers, assemble them on their corresponding boards, and crumb-coat them (see page 150),

- cakes:
- – 2½-inch round, 3½ inches high
- – 4-inch round, 2½ inches high
- – 7-inch round, 2½ inches high
- gum paste (page 154)
- egg-crate foam pad
- colors:
- – nontoxic super pearl iridescent powder
- – peach and caramel paste
- lemon extract
- small paintbrush
- 2½-, 4-, and 7-inch round foamcore boards

- rolled fondant (page 145)
- 9-inch round plate
- scallop-edged pastry wheel
- royal icing (page 147)
- pastry bag and coupler
- tips: PME #2, PME #3
- #24-gauge, 18-inch cloth-covered white wire
- needle-nose pliers

then chill them. Cover them with pale-peach fondant and stack them on the plate.

Use the pastry wheel to cut ivory fondant (made with caramel paste color) into 8 4-by-1¼-inch strips that will run down the sides of the bottom tier. Brush the backs with a little water and attach the strips, evenly spaced, around the tier. Cut 8 3-by-1-inch strips and attach them to the middle tier, lining them up *between* the strips on the tier below. Cut 8 4-by-½-inch strips and attach them to the top tier, again lining them up between the strips on the tier below. Attach 1-inch-wide strips of fondant horizontally around the bottom edge of each tier.

Using the #3 tip, outline the edges of each strip with white royal icing. Glue pearls down the center of each vertical strip with royal icing, using ¼-inch pearls on the top tier (8 on each strip), ⁵⁄₁₆-inch pearls on the middle tier (4 on each strip), and ⅜-inch pearls on the bottom (6 on each strip). Place pearls the same size as those on the tier below around the bottom of each horizontal strip, putting larger pearls in the spaces between the strips, as shown in the photograph on page 75. Scatter pearls of all sizes around the plate, attaching them with royal icing.

Attach a ¾-inch pearl topped by a ½-inch pearl to the top of the cake, and encircle them with additional ½-inch pearls.

carat cake

This fantasy cake is adorned with April's birthstone, the diamond, represented by glittering rock candy. The candle on top is covered with diamonds made of sugar, and even the plate holding the cake slice is edible.

- cakes:
  - 4-inch round,
    1½ inches high
  - 7-inch round,
    1½ inches high
  - 9-inch round,
    1½ inches high
- 13-inch round base,
  ½ inch thick
- colors:
  caramel, pink, and
  eggshell paste
- royal icing (page 147)
- ½-inch-wide white ribbon
- white glue
- gum paste (page 154)
- 7½-inch round dessert
  plate
- cornstarch
- 4-, 7-, and 9-inch round
  foamcore boards
- X-acto knife
- measuring tape
- rolled fondant (page 145)
- ¼-inch-thick wooden
  dowels
- clear piping gel
- paintbrush
- ³/₁₆-inch-wide silver
  dragées
- tweezers
- crystal sugar
- 1½ pounds rock candy
- 1 candle, brushed with
  piping gel and covered
  with crystal sugar

In advance:

Cover the base with thinned pale-mauve royal icing (mix a small amount of caramel coloring with pink). Let dry. Glue the ribbon around the edge of the base.

To make the plate for the single cake slice, roll out eggshell-tinted gum paste ³/₁₆ inch thick and cut out a 7¾-inch circle. Place it on the back of a 7½-inch dessert plate that has been dusted with cornstarch to prevent sticking. Let the gum-paste plate dry for 24 hours, then remove it from the dessert plate and let it dry upright for another 24 hours.

To decorate:

Bake the cakes and let them cool completely.

Stack and center the boards. Using the X-acto knife, cut a wedge from the center of the boards that is 5 inches wide at the curved edge of the 9-inch board (**1**). Reserve the cutouts to use as boards for the individual cake slice.

Fill the tiers and assemble them on their corresponding boards. Cut a slice from each cake tier along the cut edges of the boards and assemble the slices on the reserved cutouts. Crumb-coat both cakes, including the cut areas (see page 150), and chill them.

Cover the cakes with caramel-colored fondant, easing the fondant carefully over the cut areas. Insert dowels in the largest tier and attach it to the base using royal icing. Stack the other tiers on top of the bottom tier.

Stack the 3 cut cake slices on the gum-paste plate and insert a sharpened dowel through all 3 layers (**2**).

Brush piping gel along the bottom ½ inch of each tier—including the tiers on the "slice"—and attach two rows of dragées with the tweezers, then add another dragée above every fourth one in the upper row. Brush piping gel over all of each cake, except for the cut surfaces, and sprinkle with crystal sugar.

Brush piping gel on the cut sides of both cakes and on the base just below the cut area. Starting at the base, stack rock candy on the piping gel. Place the candle on top of the cake and encircle it with dragées.

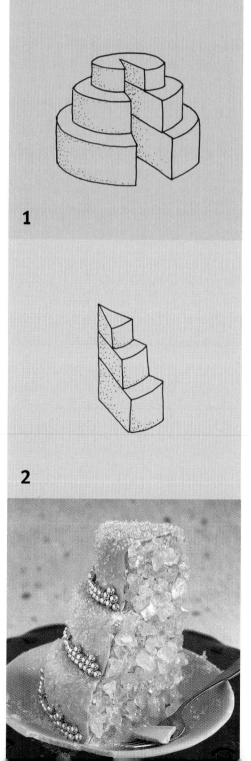

1

2

assorted
party cakes

arlene's party cake

You don't need to have a friend named Arlene to make this cake: I've designed a whole alphabet so you can combine letters to spell any name you wish.

- cakes:
  - 3¼-inch square, 1½ inches high
  - 4¾-inch square, 1½ inches high
  - 6¼-inch square, 1¾ inches high
- 10-inch-square base, ½ inch thick
- royal icing (page 147)
- colors: pink, golden-yellow, ice-blue, teal, leaf-green, Christmas red, and royal-blue paste
- ½-inch-wide peach ribbon
- white glue
- wax paper or silicone-coated unbleached parchment paper
- pastry bags and couplers
- tips: PME #2, PME #3, #233
- 3-inch-diameter foamcore circle
- Styrofoam cone, 3 inches high and 3 inches wide at the base
- rolled fondant (page 145)
- gum paste (page 154)
- pizza cutter
- 3¼-, 4¾-, and 6¼-inch-square foamcore boards
- ¼-inch-thick wooden dowels
- palette knife

In advance:

Cover the base with thinned peach (a mixture of pink and golden-yellow) royal icing. Let dry. Glue the peach ribbon around the edge.

Make the royal-icing plaques (**1–2**), using the run-in-sugar technique (page 170). The colors you will be using for the letters are pink, yellow, green (made with ice-blue, teal, and leaf-green), and red.

You'll need to make a plaque for the name of the person whose birthday it is, using the alphabet in patterns **4** and **5** — unless, of course, the person's name happens to be Arlene, in which case you can use pattern **3**. Enlarge all of the patterns (**1**, **2**, and **3** or **4** and **5**). Sketch the name on a piece of paper, using the alphabet as a guide and making sure that the final design does not exceed the width of the cake's bottom tier. Overlap the letters as needed. Place all of the patterns (**1**, **2**, and **3** or **4** and **5**) on the back of a cookie sheet and tape a sheet of wax or parchment paper on top. Outline 4 HAPPYs and 4 BIRTHDAYs with yellow royal icing and fill in one of each with pink, then repeat with yellow, green, and red royal icing using the #2 tip. Outline and fill in the name 4 times the same way. Let the plaques dry for about 2 hours. Then, with the #3 tip, outline the left edges and some of the right edges of the letters with blue, as shown in the photograph on page 83. Using the #2 tip, pipe the remaining edges with adjacent lines of pink and yellow icing. Let the designs dry overnight.

To make the hat for the top of the cake, first attach the 3-inch foamcore circle to the bottom of the cone, so that no Styrofoam comes in contact with the cake. Cover the Styrofoam cone with blue-green (a mixture of ice-blue, royal-blue, and leaf-green) fondant. Roll a 1/8-inch-thick cord of teal fondant, brush one side with a little water, and wrap it in a spiral around the cone. Cut a 1/2-inch-wide strip of peach fondant and wrap it around the cone, leaving about 1/4 inch on either side of the teal spiral. Using the #2 tip and pink royal icing, pipe rows of dots on the blue and peach areas of the hat.

To make the ribbons for the top of the hat, roll out some white gum paste and use the pizza cutter to cut it into 2½-by-3/16-inch strips. Cut one end of each strip diagonally and pinch the other end. Curve and twist the strips to resemble ribbons. Let dry overnight on a cookie sheet.

To decorate:
Bake the cakes and let them cool completely. Fill the tiers and assemble them on their corresponding boards. Crumb-coat the tiers (see page 150) and chill them. Cover each tier with peach fondant. Stack the tiers on the base and place the hat on top of the cake, gluing everything together with royal icing.

Carefully remove the letters from the paper by sliding a thin palette knife under them. Attach them to the sides of each tier with royal icing. Use the #3 tip to fill in any exposed areas along the bottom edge of each tier — that is, any parts not covered by the letters — with dots of peach royal icing. Decorate the rest of the cake with evenly spaced dots. Using the #233 tip, pipe a border along the bottom of the hat with white royal icing.

Attach the pinched ends of the ribbons to the top of the hat with royal icing.

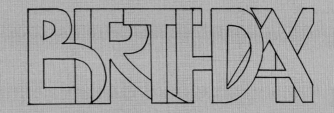

1 enlarge 182%   **2** enlarge 182%

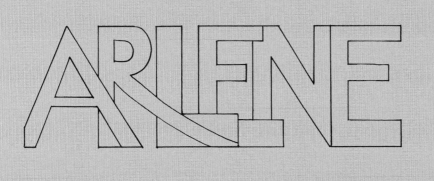
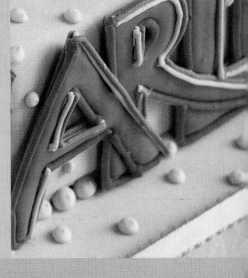

3 enlarge 182%

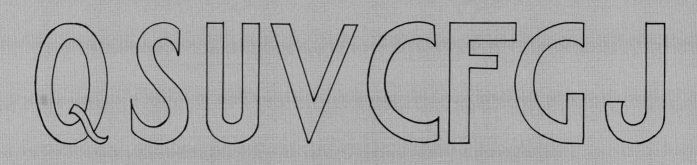

4 enlarge 182%

5 enlarge 182%

groundhog day cake

SERVES 30

Hats off to Punxsutawney Phil and all the other groundhogs whose shadow sightings make February 2 birthdays (including mine) so memorable! Every part of this cuddly cake is edible, including the dirt.

- cakes:
  3 6-inch round, 2 3 inches high and 1 4 inches high (10 inches total)
- 6-inch hexagonal cake pan
- 3 6-inch and 2 18-inch round foamcore boards
- X-acto knife
- white glue
- pastry bags and couplers
- tips: #8, PME #2, #233
- royal icing (page 147)
- colors:
- delphinium-blue, yellow, Wilton Winnie-the-Pooh Gold, green, and brown paste
- royal-blue, purple, blue, yellow, orange, and green airbrush paint
- nontoxic blue, yellow, and black powder
- ½-inch-wide white ribbon
- gum paste (page 154)
- pizza cutter
- egg-crate foam pad
- 2 sugar molds, one made in a 1-inch and the other in a 1½-inch fluted biscuit cutter (page 174)
- candle
- 1 gum-paste primrose and 3 primrose leaves on wires (page 160)
- ¼-inch-thick wooden dowels
- rolled fondant (page 145)
- small serrated knife
- buttercream icing (page 143)
- small paintbrush
- gum-paste ball tool
- 10 Oreo cookies (with filling removed), crushed

In advance:

To make the base, outline the 6-inch hexagonal cake pan in the center of one of the 18-inch boards. Make 6 more outlines of the hexagon around the first one (**1**). Cut the outer edges with the X-acto knife. Glue the cut board onto the second 18-inch board. When the glue is dry, cut around the second board to match the first.

Using the #8 tip, pipe delphinium-blue royal icing around the hexagonal outlines. Fill in the areas between the lines with thinned yellow-ocher royal icing (made from yellow, Winnie-the-Pooh Gold, and green). Let dry. Glue the ribbon around the edge of the base.

Roll green gum paste ¹⁄₁₆ inch thick. With the pizza cutter, cut blades of grass and let them dry on the egg-crate foam.

Glue the sugar molds together with royal icing. Using the #2 tip, pipe dots of yellow royal icing around the edges and bases of the molds. Attach the candle to the top and pipe dots around it with royal icing.

Make a blue primrose and 2 leaves on wires (see page 160).

To decorate:

Bake the cakes and let them cool completely. Fill the tiers and assemble them on their boards. Insert dowels in one of the 3-inch-high tiers. Using the cake pan as a guide, cut 2 6-inch circles of fondant. Place one circle on top of the doweled tier, then add the second 3-inch tier and the second fondant circle. With the serrated knife, carefully shave off the sides of the cake a little at a time, at a slight angle, so the bottom is ½ inch narrower than the top on all sides. Crumb-coat the cake (see page 150) and chill it.

To make a pattern for the tiles, cut a strip of paper the same height as the cake and as long as the circumference of the cake. Fold the paper in half, then in half again, and so on, until the folds are as wide as you want the tiles to be. Fold the paper horizontally as shown in figure **2**. Cut out one section and trim ¼ inch from all sides to allow space for the buttercream "grout."

Roll out the fondant ⅛ inch thick. Using the pattern, cut out fondant tiles with the pizza cutter. Attach the tiles to the tiers, keeping them ⅛ inch apart and working around horizontally first, then up the sides.

With the #8 tip, pipe lines of delphinium-blue buttercream between the tiles.

Mix royal-blue airbrush color with a small amount of purple. Outline the designs (**2**) with a small paintbrush, then fill them in with pale blue, as shown in the photograph on page 87.

Carve the 4-inch-high tier to shape the groundhog, using **3** as a guide. Don't worry about your sculpting being less than perfect — you can make adjustments as you pipe the fur. With the #233 tip, pipe the fur with brown buttercream icing. Attach the sugar-mold cake to the top edge of the pot with royal icing. Shape some fondant into paws and attach them with royal icing to both the groundhog and the sugar mold, so that he

appears to be holding it, as shown in the photograph. With the #233 tip, pipe brown fur over each paw. Make the eyes and nose from black gum paste, using the curved ball tool to carve the nostrils, and attach them with royal icing.

Insert a sharpened 10-inch-long dowel through the groundhog's head, pushing it in all the way to the base of the cake.

Fill around the top to the brim of the pot with cookie crumbs. Insert the wires of the flower and the leaves in the groundhog's head. Sprinkle cookie crumbs all over the top of the head. Attach the gum-paste grass around the pot with dots of royal icing; arrange some blades lying flat and others pointing upward. Sprinkle cookie crumbs around the base, if desired.

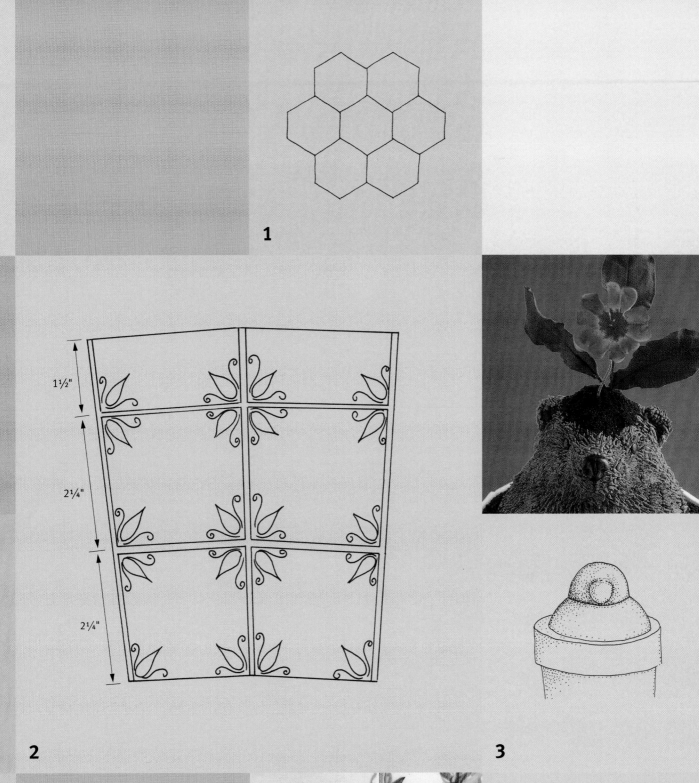

1

1½"

2¼"

2¼"

2

3

the doctor's bag

Whether your guest of honor is a medical practitioner or just a hypochondriac, this cake will make everyone say "Ahh!" You can easily replicate the look of old leather with chocolate fondant.

- cakes:
  3 13-by-9-inch rectangles,
  2 inches high
- chocolate rolled fondant
  (page 145)
- pizza cutter
- cornstarch
- gum paste (page 154)
- colors:
  - nontoxic silver iridescent
    and black powder
  - flesh and brown paste
  - dark-brown and black
    airbrush paint
- lemon extract
- paintbrushes
- ridged rolling pin
- toothpick
- Mike + Ike candies
- 20-inch round foil-covered
  base, ½ inch high

- pastry bag and coupler
- tip: #7
- royal icing (page 147)
- 2 foamcore boards,
  12 by 5½ inches each
- ¼-inch-thick wooden
  dowels
- small serrated knife
- textured plastic sheet
  (such as a fluorescent
  light cover) or silicone
  impression mat available
  from Sunflower (see
  "Sources")
- airbrush

In advance:

Make the frame of the bag and the 2 handles out of chocolate fondant. Roll out the fondant ¼ inch thick. Using pattern **1**, cut out the 2 pieces of the frame with the pizza cutter. Roll out fondant ½ inch thick and, using pattern **2**, cut out the 2 handles. They should be rounded at the top and flatter on the sides. Let all of the pieces dry on a surface dusted with cornstarch to prevent sticking.

Use white gum paste and pattern **3** to make 2 clasps. Follow patterns **4–7** to create the stethoscope, also made from gum paste. Let dry 24 hours. Mix silver iridescent powder with lemon extract and paint the clasp, the rings (1 2-inch-wide gum-paste ring, cut into 4 equal pieces), and the parts of the stethoscope that are silver in the photograph. Mix black powdered color with lemon extract and paint the areas that should be black.

To make the bandages, roll out some gum paste ⅛ inch thick. Next, roll the gum paste with the ridged rolling pin: first go over it in one direction, then turn the paste 90 degrees and roll the pin perpendicularly over the first set of ridges to create a woven look. Using the pizza cutter, cut a strip 12 inches long and 1¼ inches wide. Roll up the strip, leaving about 2 inches unrolled. Roll out more gum paste ¹⁄₁₆ inch thick and repeat the entire process, ending up with a strip 11 inches long and 2½ inches wide. Let the rolls stand on their sides to dry.

To make the Band-Aids, tint a small amount of gum paste flesh-colored and roll it out ¹⁄₁₆ inch thick. Cut 4¾-inch-wide strips, 2 of them 3 inches long and the other 2 1 inch long. The ends of the 3-inch strips should be slightly rounded. Center the 1-inch strip on top and make holes in it with a toothpick.

To make the "pills," cut the Mike + Ike candies in half crosswise and immediately join different-colored pieces together; they will stick to each other without any royal icing.

To decorate the base, divide it into 3-inch squares (**8**), piping lines with white royal icing and the #7 tip. Fill the squares with thinned white royal icing. Let dry overnight.

To decorate:
Bake the cakes and let them cool completely. Use figures **9** and **10** as a guide to cut the cakes. Fill and assemble the 13-inch layers, cut down to 12 by 5½ inches, on one of the foamcore boards, until the bottom tier is 3¾ inches high. Insert dowels and add a layer of chocolate fondant. Center the other board on top and finish filling and stacking the layers.

To bevel the top of the bag, start at the top edge and carefully shave off a little at a time, using the serrated knife. The top should measure 8 by 2 inches.

Crumb-coat the cake (see page 150) and chill it. Cover it with chocolate fondant. To give the

surface the texture of leather, press the fondant with the plastic sheet or impression mat. (I have found that plastic works better because it is stiffer; you can buy it in hardware stores that sell light covers for fluorescent bulbs.)

Attach the frame pieces and the handles to the top of the cake with brown royal icing. Attach pattern **11** pieces below the handles. Airbrush the handles and around the top and the seams of the bag with dark-brown and black airbrush colors mixed together to give the bag a weathered look. Attach the clasp (**3**) and the metal rings with royal icing.

Transfer the cake to the base and arrange the "pills" and gum-paste decorations around it, gluing them in place with royal icing.

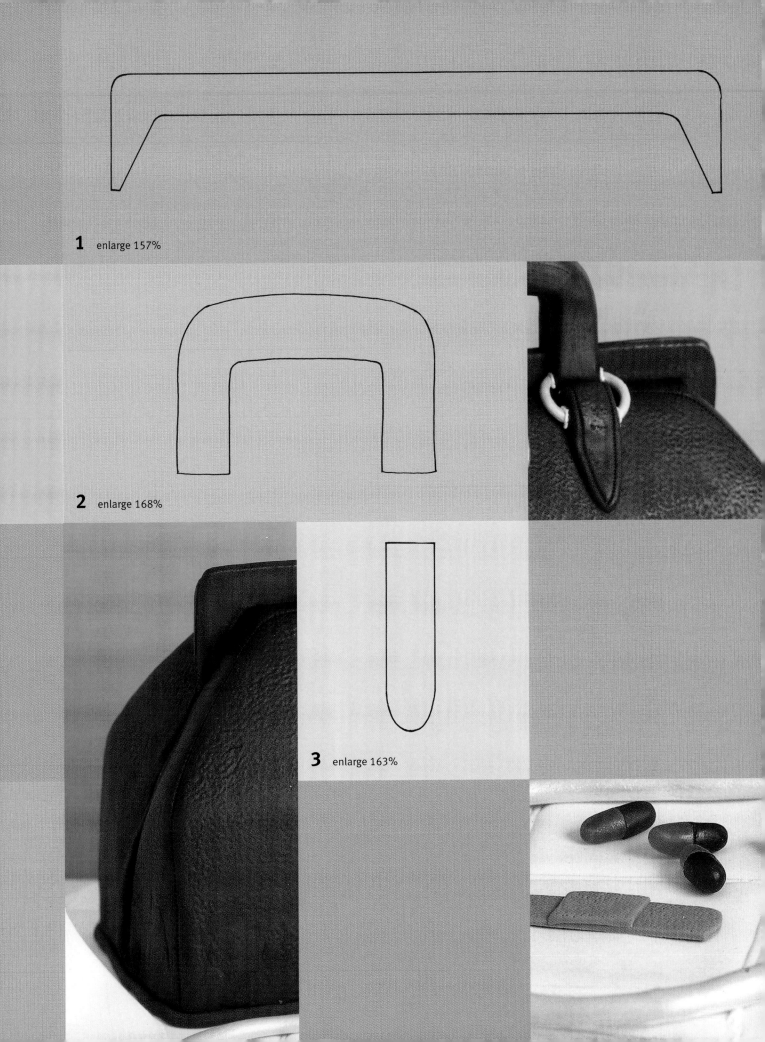

1 enlarge 157%

2 enlarge 168%

3 enlarge 163%

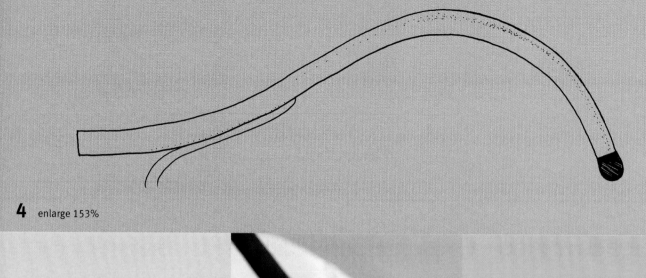

4 enlarge 153%

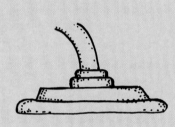

5 enlarge 120%

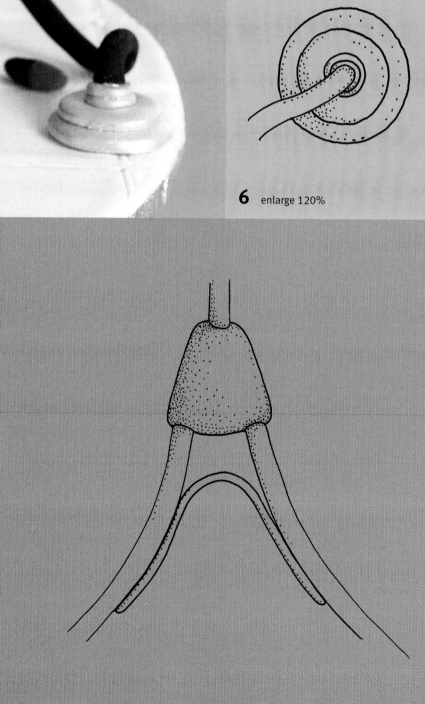

6 enlarge 120%

7 enlarge 153%

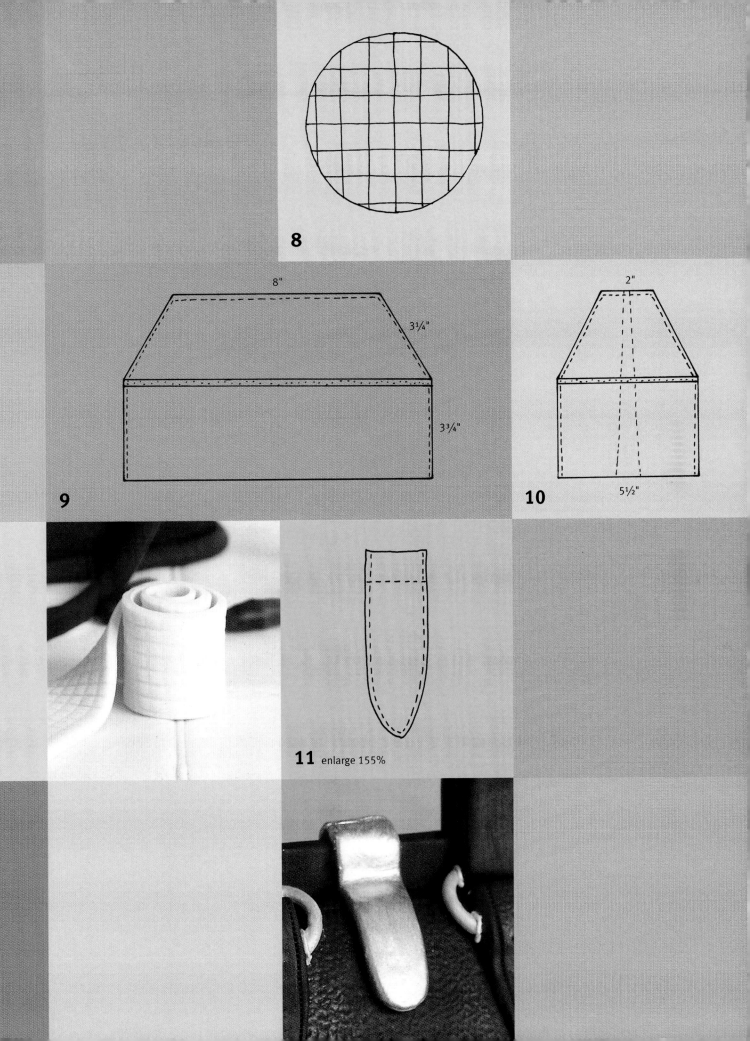

8

9

8"

3¼"

3¾"

10

2"

5½"

11 enlarge 155%

happy birthday balloon

The young at heart will love this zany balloon-shaped cake. The good thing about this cake is that it won't explode when you cut into it!

- cake:
  16-inch round,
  5 inches high
- 16-inch round foamcore board
- small serrated knife
- rolled fondant (page 145)
- oval crimpers
- colors:
- nontoxic antique white, silver, and gold iridescent powder
- egg-yellow, red, royal-blue, coral, teal, juniper-green, violet, delphinium-blue, and black paste
- red, lemon-yellow, and sunset-orange airbrush paint
- lemon extract
- clean sponge or cheese-cloth
- royal icing (page 147)
- 18-inch round foil-covered base, ½ inch high

- paintbrushes
- ridged rolling pin
- pizza cutter
- pastry bags and couplers
- tips: PME #2, PME #3
- clay gun
- airbrush
- 1½-inch-wide star cutter
- edible gold glitter
- PME gum-paste blade tool
- X-acto knife
- clear piping gel
- textured mold
- ¼-inch-thick wooden dowel
- serrated and plain tracing wheels
- scallop-edged cutter

To decorate:

Bake the cake and let it cool completely. Fill the layers and assemble them on the foamcore board. Using the serrated knife, shave off the top edge of the cake a little at a time until it is curved all around. Make vertical cuts at random intervals down to about 2 inches from the base. The shape should resemble the creased edge of a Mylar balloon (**1**). Crumb-coat the cake (see page 150) and chill it.

Cover the cake with fondant. With the crimpers, emboss a continuous border around the cake 3 inches up from the bottom.

To paint the fondant, mix antique white and silver iridescent powder with lemon extract on separate flat plates. Dip a clean sponge or a wadded-up piece of cheesecloth into one color at a time and dab it all over the cake. Transfer the cake to the base, attaching it with royal icing.

For the balloon's tie, roll out a piece of fondant and cut a 4-by-1½-inch strip. Brush one long side with water and fold it over ¼ inch. Pinch the short ends together to form a 1-inch-wide tube. Pinch the unfolded edge, leaving the folded edge round (**2**). Roll out another piece of fondant and cut a 2½-inch-long strip to wrap around the pinched end. Attach the tie to the front of the cake with royal icing.

For the fondant letters of "HAPPY BIRTHDAY," use patterns **3**–**15**. For the *B* in the center (**3**), roll 2¼-inch-thick cords of fondant, one 27 inches long and the other 15 inches long, and form the letter. Attach it to the cake with a little water. Mix silver iridescent powder with lemon extract and paint it.

For the first *H* (**4**), roll out a piece of yellow fondant ¼ inch thick and emboss it with the ridged rolling pin. Cut 2 3-by-1¼-inch strips with the pizza cutter. Mix gold powder with lemon extract and paint alternate ridges gold. Shape a 1-inch-thick ball of red fondant, pressing it slightly to flatten the bottom, and glue it to the center edges of the strips with royal icing.

For the *A* (**5**), roll out pale-blue fondant ⅛ inch thick and cut the shapes shown. Pipe blue royal icing along the edges with the #2 tip, and coral royal-icing decorations with the #3 tip, as shown in the photograph on page 94.

For the first *P* (**6**), roll long, ¼-inch-thick cords of teal fondant. Twist 2 cords at a time into 4 4-inch-long ropes and form the letter.

For the second *P* (**7**), press white fondant through the ¼-inch-circle die of the clay gun to make a 20-inch-long cord, and use it to form the letter. Spray the edges red with the airbrush, holding the nozzle parallel to the surface. Let dry.

For the *Y* (**8**), roll out a small piece of white fondant ¹⁄₁₆ inch thick. Cut a star with the 1½-inch-wide star cutter. Brush the star with clear piping gel, then sprinkle it with gold glitter. Roll out some pale juniper-green fondant ¼ inch thick. Cut the 2 triangles and emboss ridges with the blade tool, starting at the point where the longer sides meet. Cut out *V*s between the ridges

of the curved triangle with the X-acto knife. Mix gold powder with lemon extract and paint the ridges. When the paint is dry, glue the star to the points of the triangle with royal icing, as shown.

For the *I* (**9**), roll out a small piece of yellow fondant ⅛ inch thick and emboss it with the textured mold. Cut a 3-by-1-inch strip. For the dot, coil a ⅛-inch-thick cord of yellow fondant. With the airbrush, spray both pieces yellow, then switch to red, holding the nozzle parallel to the work surface.

For the *R* (**10**), roll out a ¼-inch-thick cord of yellow fondant 12 inches long and use it to form the letter. Spray the right edge orange with the airbrush.

For the *T* (**11**), roll out 1 teal and 1 violet piece of fondant, each ⅛ inch thick. Brush one side of both pieces with water and roll them together. Cut 2 8-by-1-inch strips and twist them around the dowel to dry.

For the second *H* (**12**), roll out a piece of red fondant ⅛ inch thick and cut the shape with the serrated tracing wheel. Emboss a row of stitching ⅛ inch in from the edge with the same wheel. Mix gold powder with lemon extract and paint the letter.

For the *D* (**13**), roll out a piece of pale-blue (a mixture of violet and delphinium-blue) fondant ¼ inch thick and cut the shape, pressing the edge slightly so that the surface is a little rounded. Pipe pink dots on it with the #2 tip.

For the second *A* (**14**), press yellow fondant through the ⅛-inch-circle die of the clay gun until you have about 8 8-inch-long cords. Cut 3 inches off for each side of the letter, pinch them together gently at the top, then tuck one end of the remaining bunch of 2-inch cords under the left side, allowing them to extend over the right.

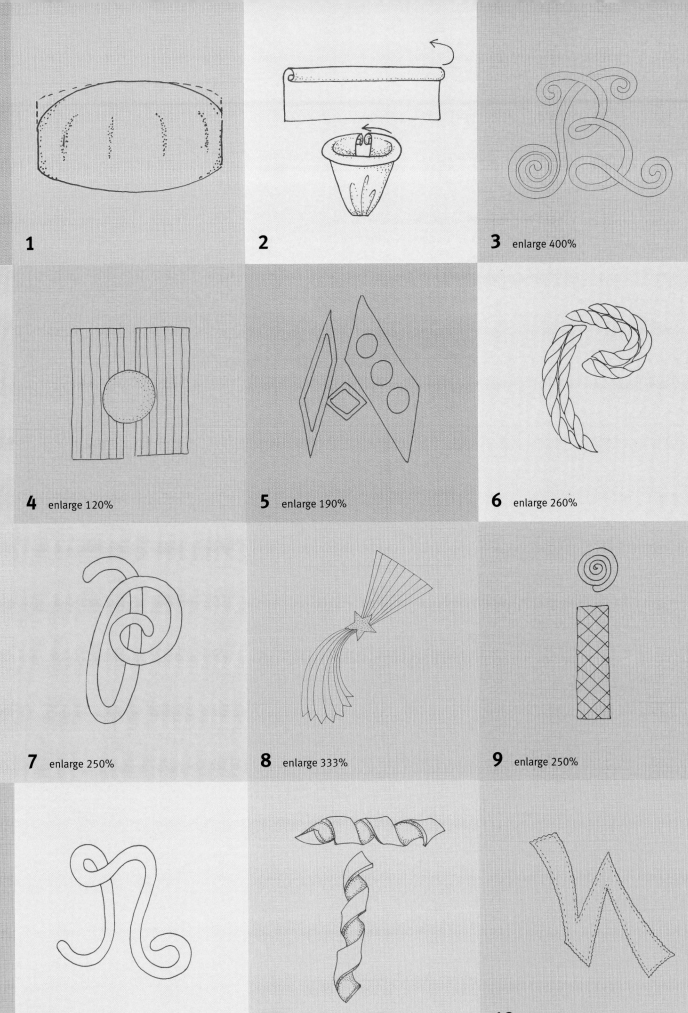

1

2

3 enlarge 400%

4 enlarge 120%

5 enlarge 190%

6 enlarge 260%

7 enlarge 250%

8 enlarge 333%

9 enlarge 250%

10 enlarge 250%

11 enlarge 250%

12 enlarge 250%

For the second *Y* (**15**), cut 2 strips of white fondant, one 3-by-1-inch and the other 2-by-½-inch, with the scallop-edged cutter. Using the #2 tip, pipe the edges with violet royal icing, then pipe black dots as shown in the photograph on page 98. Attach the strips to each other with a ½-inch-wide button of fondant, ¼ inch thick.

Glue the decorated letters to the top of the cake with royal icing.

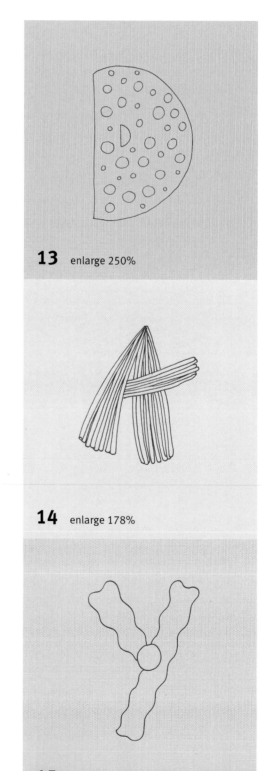

13 enlarge 250%

14 enlarge 178%

15 enlarge 210%

amy's pillow

SERVES 35 The art of ribbon weaving inspired this satiny-looking cake, which is embossed and painted to create the illusion of a woven pillow. Having a set of alphabet cutters on hand makes it easy to lend a personal touch to the cake.

- cake:
  10-inch square,
  4 inches high
- 8-inch-square foamcore board
- royal icing (page 147)
- small serrated knife
- rolled fondant (page 145)
- colors:
- willow-green paste
- nontoxic green, blue, oyster, and super pearl iridescent powder
- straight-edged tracing wheel
- flexible straightedge (such as a piece of thin cardboard)

- lemon extract
- paintbrush
- pizza cutter
- scallop-edged pastry wheel
- Ateco alphabet cutters, 1 inch long
- pastry bag and coupler
- tip: PME #2

To decorate:

Bake the cake and let it cool completely. Fill the cake, then center the board on top, attaching it with icing. Use the serrated knife to carefully shave off the top edge of the cake a little at a time until it is beveled and rounded. Invert the cake and repeat on the other side (**1**). Crumb-coat the cake (see page 150) and chill it. Cover the cake with pale-green fondant, then tuck the fondant under it to the edge of the board.

Using the tracing wheel and the straightedge, emboss lines lengthwise and crosswise over the top, as shown in figure **2**. The surface should resemble ribbons woven under and over one another. Mix the iridescent powders with lemon extract and paint the ribbons as shown, one color at a time.

To make the ruffle, roll out a 12-by-10-inch piece of white fondant ⅛ inch thick. Using the pizza cutter, cut a 12-by-2½-inch strip. Cut one of the 12-inch edges with the scallop-edged pastry wheel. With the scalloped edge facing you, use the alphabet cutters to cut out the letters of the recipient's name, running across the strip. Use the cut-out letters for the top of the cake. Brush the straight edge of the strip with a little water and attach it to the side of the cake, gently folding and ruffling the strip as you work. Prop up the bottom edge with crumpled paper towels or tissues until the strip is set. Repeat the same steps with 3 more fondant strips, positioning them around the cake. Cut the corners diagonally and fold the cut edges under to make the ruffle appear continuous.

With the #2 tip, pipe a snail trail (see page 152) of white royal icing around the seam where the ruffle meets the cake. Apply less pressure to the pastry bag and pipe smaller trails around the edges of the cut-out letters on the ruffle and around the top of the cake. Pipe 3 small dots on each point of the scalloped edge of the ruffle. Decorate the top of the cake as desired, attaching the reserved letters with a dab of royal icing.

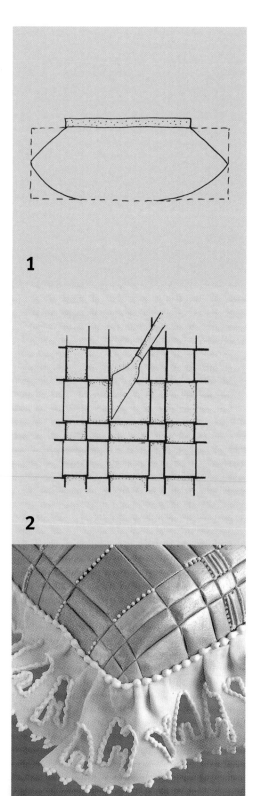

1

2

the great crate cake

SERVES 165

- cakes:
- 7-by-4-inch rectangle,
  3½ inches high (made in
  an 8-inch square pan)
- 8-inch square,
  4¾ inches high
- 12-by-10½-inch rectangle,
  7 inches high (made in
  a 12-inch square pan)
- foamcore for the box
  on top
- X-acto knife
- white glue
- chocolate and white rolled
  fondant (page 145)
- 16-by-13½-inch base,
  ¾ inch high
- pizza cutter
- tip: #9
- colors:
- nontoxic silver iridescent
  powder
- brown and black airbrush
  paint

- lemon extract
- paintbrush
- ruler
- tracing wheel
- gum paste (page 154)
- ¼-inch-thick wooden
  dowels
- airbrush
- clear piping gel
- yellow edible glitter
- thin cardboard for stencil
- scissors
- 2 foamcore boards, one
  7 by 4 inches and the
  other 8 inches square
- nontoxic felt-tip marker

SERVES 165

When I make cakes that are to be shipped to customers around the country, I pack them in crates that look just like those pictured here. The difference is that these crates are actually the tiers of a cake, which I made for my good friend and handyman, "Sudsy O'Riley."

In advance:

Make the small foamcore box and lid that will go on top of the cake and hold the candle. The box measures 5¼ inches long by 3¾ inches wide by 1¾ inches deep. Cut out the 5 pieces with the X-acto knife, glue the edges together, and let dry.

The box, the base, and the cake are all covered with different shades of marbleized brown fondant, which is then sprayed with the airbrush to create the look of wood grain. To marbleize the fondant, make 3 shades of brown fondant by mixing varying amounts of white and chocolate fondant together. When you are ready to cover the base, roll some of each color into a thick cord and then twist the 3 cords together. Roll them into a rope and knead them together until they are slightly blended. Then, as you roll out the fondant, you will see the various shades appear.

Cover the base and the foamcore box with fondant. Use the pizza cutter to cut ½-inch-wide strips of marbleized fondant. Brush one side of each strip with water and attach the strips to all the edges of the box. Emboss nails around the strips with the top of the #9 tip. Mix silver iridescent powder with lemon extract and paint the nail heads. With the ruler and the tracing wheel, emboss straight lines 1½ inches apart across the base and the lid to resemble wooden boards, as shown in the photograph on page 105. For the candle, marbleize a small amount of gum paste, roll it into a cord, and wrap it around a dampened dowel.

With the airbrush, spray thin parallel lines of brown over the marbling to darken it (**1**). Place the candle inside the box and attach the ends to the top and bottom. Form a small piece of gum paste in the shape of a flame and attach it to the top of the box, just above the candle. Brush it with piping gel and sprinkle it with yellow glitter.

To decorate:

Bake the cakes and let them cool completely. Fill the tiers and assemble them on their corresponding boards. Crumb-coat the tiers (see page 150) and chill them. Marbleize and roll out the fondant to cover the tiers as you did for the base. Insert dowels in the 2 larger tiers. Cut ¾-inch-wide strips of marbleized fondant for the top cake tier, 1-inch-wide strips for the middle tier, and 1½-inch-wide strips for the bottom tier. Attach them to form a frame around all the sides of all of the tiers by brushing water on the backs. Emboss nails randomly around the strips and paint them silver. Stack the cake tiers and insert a sharpened dowel all the way through the center of the cake to the base. Airbrush the wood grain.

Cut the stencil (**2**) out of the center of a sheet of thin cardboard. Place the stencil on the side of the bottom tier and spray it with the airbrush to form the word FRAGILE in black letters on all

sides. Using a photocopier, reduce the stencil by 25 percent (from 6 by 1½ inches to 4½ by 1⅛ inches). Repeat on all the sides of the remaining tiers and the lid.

Roll out some gum paste ¹⁄₁₆ inch thick and cut out the stickers with the pizza cutter. Mark the stickers as shown in the photograph on page 105. Roll more gum paste ⅛ inch thick and cut out the address sticker for the recipient. Write the labels on the stickers with the nontoxic marking pen.

To make the rope, roll 2 long cords of light-brown gum paste ¼ inch thick and twist them together. Brush one side with a little water and then drape the rope over the tiers, using the photograph as a guide. Tuck the ends over the intersecting ropes to resemble knots. Fray some of the ends on the top tier with scissors.

Place the box on top of the cake and attach the lid to one edge of the top cake tier with royal icing. Attach the gum-paste stickers as shown.

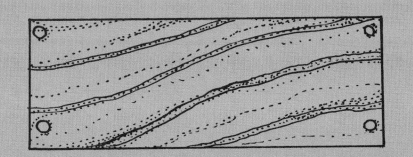

1

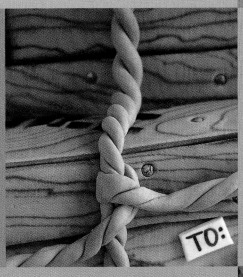

TO:

FRAGILE

2 enlarge 140%

kid's krispy kake

Although it looks like a fantasy castle in some mythical kingdom, this birthday "cake," made from Rice Krispies Treats and candy, would be right at home at any child's birthday party. Plus, there's no baking!

In advance:

Make the Rice Krispies Treats "cake" layers in the pans indicated and 8 cones in the greased tree molds. Stack the layers on a cake stand. They will stick to each other, so it's not necessary to "glue" them together with icing (**1**).

Tint some royal icing with Winnie-the-Pooh Gold until it's the color of Rice Krispies, then pipe a dot on the back of each piece of candy to glue it onto the cake. Glue an evenly spaced row of blue M&Ms around the top layer, 2 inches up from the base, positioning each piece of candy above a recessed groove in the layer below. Just beneath the first row, glue on another row, this one of gold M&Ms. At the base, glue an evenly spaced row of purple M&Ms to the side of the cake. Between each piece of candy, glue a gold M&M to the top of the ridge in the layer below.

Mark 8 points around the base of the molded layer that line up with the recesses in the petal layer. At each of these points, glue 2 small peach gumballs, not quite touching, to the side of the cake. Glue a small pink gumball on top, centered, and a pink M&M in front.

- layers:
  - 5-inch round, 3½ inches high, made in a metal bowl
  - 7-inch round, 2½ inches high, made in a 9-inch Bundt or fancy ring-mold pan
  - 10-inch round, 3 inches high
  - 14-inch petal, 2 inches high
- 9 recipes Rice Krispies Treats (found on boxes of Rice Krispies cereal)
- 8 Wilton tree molds
- cake stand (optional)
- royal icing (page 147)
- Wilton Winnie-the-Pooh Gold paste food coloring
- pastry bag and coupler
- tip: PME #2

- 60 light-blue, 50 gold, 100 purple, 60 pink, and 25 dark-green M&Ms
- 16 peach, 8 pink, 22 yellow, 16 orange, 22 blue, and 10 green ½-inch gumballs
- 4 *each* green, light-green, rose, and light-pink 1-inch gumballs
- wooden skewers
- 1 red 1⅛-inch gumball
- toothpicks
- 8 mini rice cakes

Assemble the cones. For each cone, stack a small yellow, a small orange, and a medium light- or dark-green gumball on a wooden skewer. Insert the skewer into the top of the cone. Pierce a rose-colored gumball with a toothpick and insert it into the bottom of the tree. Between the gumball clusters, lined up with the widest part of the bottom layer, insert the skewers near the top edge of the 10-inch layer until the red gumballs are resting on the cake. Glue a small blue gumball on both sides and in front. Just below, glue 3 dark-green M&Ms to the side (a row of 2 with 1 below). Glue a pink M&M in the center.

Between these clusters and below the pink clusters, glue small yellow gumballs about an inch down from the top edge. At the base of this layer, glue a border of purple M&Ms. Above every fourth candy, glue a blue M&M, and between them glue gold M&Ms about ¼ inch above the border.

On the petal layer, stack 2 blue M&Ms at the widest part of each petal. On the side, in each recess, glue on a vertical row of pink, blue, and pink M&Ms, ending with a green gumball. On both sides, glue on a pink M&M halfway down the side. Glue a purple M&M on the outer edge of each petal. Glue the rice cakes to the cake under the purple M&Ms. Decorate each mini rice cake with a yellow gumball glued ¼ inch from one edge, then an orange gumball, then a blue M&M. With the yellow candy on top, stack a small yellow, a small orange, a medium rose, a large red, a small green, a small blue, and a small green gumball on a wooden skewer. Insert the skewer in the top of the cake. Glue 6 pink M&Ms at an angle around the bottom gumball. If desired, decorate the base of the cake stand with yellow, blue, and orange gumballs.

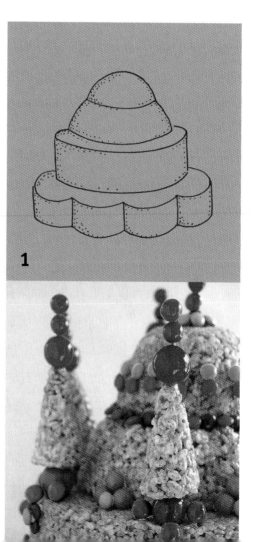

1

royal chess set

SERVES 125

This fanciful chess set is fit for a king or a queen. The chess pieces, constructed from sugar molds and encrusted with jewels made of piping gel, sit atop a cake chessboard. An avid player won't be able to decide whether to cut the cake or to checkmate.

- cake:
  18-inch square,
  2½ inches high
- 20-inch-square base,
  ½ inch high
- royal icing (page 147)
- ½-inch-wide white ribbon
- white glue
- white and chocolate
  rolled fondant (page 145)
- colors:
- October orange, chestnut,
  flesh, royal-blue, violet,
  grape-violet, egg-yellow,
  brown, willow-green,
  kelly-green, melon, and
  teal paste
- nontoxic white and gold
  iridescent powder
- orange and red liquid
  food coloring

- ⅝- and 1-inch biscuit
  cutters
- pizza cutter
- lemon extract
- paintbrushes
- pastry bag and coupler
- tip: PME #2
- clear piping gel
- 18-inch-square foamcore
  board
- toothpick
- tracing wheel
- ³⁄₁₆-inch gold dragées
- ¼-inch silver dragées

MOLD	SIZE (width x height)	NUMBER NEEDED
King		
Round fluted biscuit cutter	1½″ x ¾″	2
Square plain tart pan	1″ x ½″	4
Round fluted tart pan	2½″ x 1″	4
Foil mini-tart pan	2″	2
Round fluted tart pan	3″	4

(continued)

In advance:

Cover the base with thinned white royal icing and let dry. Glue the ribbon around the edge.

Make the chess pieces from the sugar molds. One set will be brightly colored, the other brown and white. There will be 2 kings, one for each side; 2 queens; 4 bishops; 4 rooks; 4 knights; and 16 pawns.

Mix the colors for the rolled fondant. For the orange color, combine October orange, chestnut, and flesh colors. For the blue, mix royal-blue and violet; for the yellow, mix egg-yellow and brown; for the purple, use grape-violet; for the turquoise, mix willow-, kelly-green, melon, and teal; and for the green, mix willow- and kelly-green and melon. Cover the molds for each piece with colored fondant, brushing the fondant with a little water first to make it adhere to the sugar. Use the detail photographs on pages 112–113 as a guide.

Queen

Oval fluted tart pan	2″ x ½″	2
Round fluted tart pan	2½″ x ¾″	4
Heart cutter	1″	2
Blossom cutter	1½″	2

Bishop

Round plain tart pan	1¾″ x ½″	4
Foil mini-tart pan	2″	4
Large rose tip #127		4
Large Wilton lily nail		4

Knight

Square fluted tart pan	1″ x ½″	8
Triangle plain tart pan	1¾″ x ½″	4
Round fluted tart pan	1¾″ x ½″	4
Large Wilton lily nail		4
Round straight tart pan	1½″	4

Rook

Round straight biscuit cutter	½″ x 1½″	4
Round fluted tart pan	1½″ x ½″	12
Round straight biscuit cutter	¾″ x ¼″	4
Round tart mold	1½″ x ¾″	4

Pawn

Triangle plain tart pan	1¾″ x ½″	16
Round fluted tart pan	1½″ x ½″	16
Large Wilton lily nail		16

Build each piece, starting at the bottom and gluing each section to the next with royal icing (**1**–**6**). Always allow the royal icing to dry before adding the next piece. In addition to the sugar molds, use the ⅝-, 1-, and 1½-inch biscuit cutters to cut out disks of fondant for the queens, the bishops, the rooks, and the knights, and use the pizza cutter to cut the 1-inch squares for the pawns. To assemble the brown and white pieces, alternate white and chocolate fondant as shown in the photograph.

When the pieces are assembled, let them set for a few hours before decorating them, to allow the royal icing to harden.

Mix white powdered color with lemon extract and paint the iridescent sections as shown in the individual photographs. Using the #2 tip, pipe the royal-icing decorations. Let dry, then mix gold powder with lemon extract and paint. Pipe dots of colored piping gel as shown.

To decorate:

Bake the cake and let it cool completely. Fill the layers and assemble them on the board. Crumb-coat the cake (see page 150) and chill it. Cover it with fondant. Transfer the cake to the base, gluing it in place with royal icing.

Divide each edge into 8 equal sections and mark them off with a toothpick. Use the tracing wheel to emboss free-form wavy lines across the surface of the cake, running from each mark on one edge to the corresponding mark on the opposite edge. The lines should curve but not cross. Repeat the same steps on the other side, embossing from the marks on the perpendicular edges until the surface is covered in a wavy checkerboard pattern. Emboss wavy parallel lines inside some of the squares. All the lines within a particular square should go in only one direction, but you may vary the directions among the squares.

Now paint the squares, alternating white and colors as shown in the photograph on page 111. Mix each color with lemon extract before painting. Let the surface dry.

Pipe a line of piping gel along one edge of the cake. Fill in the line with small gold dragées, adding larger silver ones at the intersections. Continue piping and applying dragées until all the lines are covered. Attach larger dragées around the border of the cake.

1

Queens

3

Kings

2

Bishops

4

Rooks

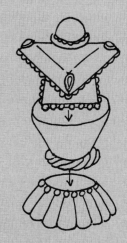

6

Knights

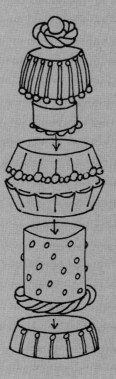

5

Pawns

karlyn's birthday bag

SERVES 20

Some of the guests at your party will wonder who left her pretty handbag on the dessert table, while others will ask, "So, where's the cake?"

- cakes:
- – 7-inch round, 2 inches high
- – 6-inch round, 2 inches high
- – 4-inch round, 2 inches high
- 6-inch round foamcore board
- serrated knife
- rolled fondant (page 145)
- pizza cutter
- colors: nontoxic silver, blue, white, and avocado-green iridescent powder
- lemon extract
- small paintbrushes
- pastry bags and couplers
- tips: PME #1.5, PME #2
- royal icing (page 147)
- gum paste (page 154)
- clay gun

To decorate:

Bake the cakes and let them cool completely. Fill the layers and assemble them on the board. Using a serrated knife, carefully shave away the sides of the cake a little at a time until the thickest part, just above the base, is 6½ inches in diameter, and the top is 3 inches in diameter. Crumb-coat the cake (see page 150) and chill it. Cover the cake with fondant, letting it drape over the tiers and tucking it in at the base while keeping the folds that form naturally.

Cut a ½-inch-wide strip of fondant with the pizza cutter. Brush one long edge with water and attach it to the top edge of the cake, forming an upright collar (**1**). Place crumpled tissues on top of the cake or insert toothpicks to hold the folds in place. Let the fondant set.

Mix silver iridescent powder with lemon extract and paint the cake, including the inside of the collar.

With the #2 tip, pipe the royal-icing flowers, stems, and leaves, using figures **2**, **3**, and **4** as guides. Use the #1.5 tip to fill in the petals with lines of icing. Paint the stems with blue iridescent powder mixed with lemon extract. Paint blue and silver highlights on the flowers and leaves, leaving parts of the piping white.

To make the tasseled rope, twist 2 12-inch-long cords of gum paste together. Brush the seam of the collar with water and wrap the rope around it. Extend a 5-inch and a 6-inch rope down the side of the cake as shown in the photograph on page 114, attaching them with a little water. Twist 2 ½-inch-long cords of fondant together and attach them to the juncture of the ropes with a little water so they resemble a knot.

Make the tassels by pressing softened fondant through the multiholed die of the clay gun to form ¾-inch-long strands. Attach a tassel to the end of each rope with water. Cover the seams between the ropes and the tassels with small cords of fondant. Mix the avocado-green powder with lemon extract and paint the ropes and tassels.

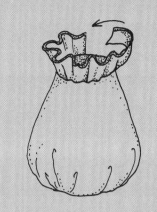

1

2

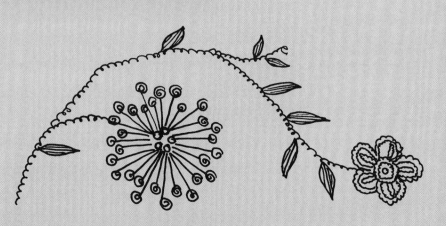

3

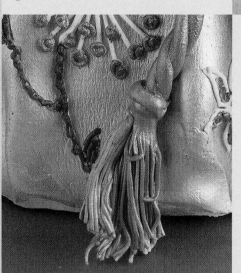

4

art deco cake

SERVES 25 The restored art deco hotels of Miami's South Beach district gave me the idea for this stylized cake. Their ornamental details and sunny pastels, captured here in royal icing, set just the right mood for a birthday celebration.

In advance:
Cover the base with thinned sky-blue and orange royal icing, as shown in figure **1**. Let dry. Glue the ribbon around the edge.

To decorate:
Bake the cake and let it cool completely. Use the foamcore boards as templates, placing them on top of the cake and cutting out the squares with the serrated knife. The height of the tiers will increase in ¼-inch increments from top to bottom, from ¼ inch for the topmost square of fondant to 2¼ inches for the bottom tiers. Fill the tiers and assemble them on their corresponding boards. Crumb-coat the tiers (see page 150) and chill them.

To cover the tiers, knead caramel (to make beige), violet (to make lavender), sky-blue, and orange paste colors into separate pieces of fondant. Starting with the largest tier, cut 2 strips each of beige and lavender to the same measure-

- cake:
  24-by-18-inch,
  1 inch high
- 8-inch square base,
  ½ inch high
- royal icing (page 147)
- colors:
- sky-blue, October orange,
  caramel, violet, lemon-
  yellow, leaf-green, forest-
  green, delphinium-blue,
  and pink paste
- nontoxic pink powder
- ½-inch-wide blue ribbon
- white glue
- 2-, 3-, 4-, 4½-, 5-, 5½-,
  and 6-inch-square foam-
  core boards

- small serrated knife
- rolled fondant (page 145)
- ¼-inch-thick wooden
  dowel
- pastry bags and couplers
- tips: PME #2, PME #3, #5,
  #8
- lemon extract
- small paintbrush
- Wilton magenta wavy
  sparkler candle (optional)

ments as the sides of the cake, and attach them to opposite sides. Using figure **2** as a guide, attach blue and orange fondant to the top of each tier. Stack the tiers as shown in figure **2** and insert a sharpened dowel all the way through the center of the cake to the base. For the top, make a 2-inch square of orange fondant, ¼ inch thick, and attach it to the highest tier.

Turn the cake so that one of the orange sides is facing you. Using the #8 tip, pipe a line of yellow royal icing from the top layer down the right corners of each tier (**3**). Pipe 2 more lines on each side of the first line. With the #5 tip, pipe another line next to the outermost #8 lines. Then pipe another line, still using the #5 tip, on top of the first #8 line. Next, overpipe the last line with a #3 line, then with a #2 line. Pipe a #8 line of yellow icing horizontally along the inside and outside edges. Pipe a wavy line horizontally about ½ inch above the bottom edge of each tier and on the base, and a zigzag line across the top edge. Overpipe all of these lines, except the outer edge, with a #3 line.

Turn the cake and repeat on the other orange side.

Now turn the cake to the blue side. With the #8 tip, pipe dots of green (mixing leaf and forest green) icing along the top edge and down the right corners of the tiers. Turn the cake and repeat on the opposite side. Pipe 2 adjacent lines of green icing along the border of each blue tier, the first with the #8 tip and the second with the #5 tip. Extend the border of the bottom tier to the edge of the base.

Use the #5 tip to decorate the tiers and base of the blue sides with delphinium-blue icing and the orange sides with yellow icing, using the photograph on page 120 as a guide. With the #2 tip, overpipe pale-yellow icing on the yellow piping and along alternate lines of the yellow border.

Mix pink powdered color with lemon extract and paint the tiers on the orange sides, leaving the areas between the piping and the edges beige. Attach a circle of pink fondant to the top of the cake and insert the candle.

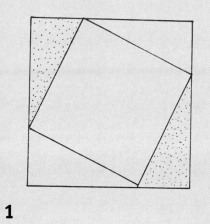

1

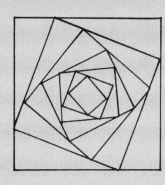

2

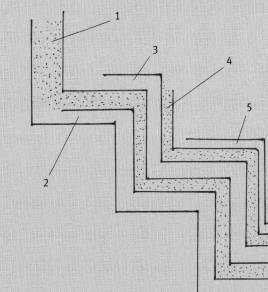

3

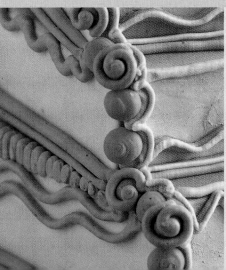

cherry
pie
purse

I wanted this cake to look like a purse that Judith Lieber might create. She designs rhinestone-studded evening bags in charming disguises (one of my favorites resembles a watermelon slice). In this faux purse, the cherry-pie filling is made of piping-gel dots to give the illusion of rhinestones.

- cake:
  14-inch round, 1 inch
  high, cut into fifths
- gum paste (page 154)
- colors:
- red, green, and brown
  paste
- nontoxic cranberry and
  gold iridescent powder
- orange, blue, and red
  liquid food coloring
- gum-paste umbrella tool
- Wilton leaf cutter
- toothpick or veining tool
- royal icing (page 147)
- lemon extract
- paintbrush
- 7-by-6-inch wedge-
  shaped foamcore (⅕ of a
  14-inch round board)

- X-acto knife
- rolled fondant (page 145)
- clear piping gel
- ¼- and ³⁄₁₆-inch silver
  dragées
- pizza cutter
- ³⁄₁₆-inch gold dragées
- tweezers
- pastry bag and coupler
- tip: PME #2

In advance:

To make the gum-paste cherries, roll red gum paste into ¾-inch balls. Indent the tops with the umbrella tool. Use the leaf cutter to cut pieces of green gum paste into 1-inch-long leaves, ⅛ inch thick. Emboss veins in the leaves with a toothpick or veining tool. Let dry.

Attach a leaf to the top of each cherry with a dot of green royal icing (see photograph on page 125). Pipe a short brown royal icing stem in front of the base of each leaf with #2 tip. Let dry. Mix cranberry powdered color with lemon extract and paint the cherries. Mix gold powder and lemon extract and lightly paint the leaves.

To decorate:

Bake the cake and let it cool completely. Divide the cake into fifths (each wedge will be 7 inches long and 6 inches wide). Fill the layers and

123

assemble them on the board. Crumb-coat the cake (see page 150) and chill it. Cover the cake with fondant. Pipe a line of clear piping gel around the bottom edge and apply a row of ¼-inch silver dragées.

Cut a piece of fondant into 1¼-inch-wide strips with the pizza cutter. Roll one of the strips into a cord and attach it, folding it in a zigzag pattern, along the wide edge, so it resembles a fluted pie crust. Lay the strips diagonally on top of the cake in a lattice pattern, as on a pie. Spread clear piping gel over the top of the lattice strips and on the back of the cake and cover those areas with small gold dragées, using the tweezers if necessary.

Mix clear piping gel with orange food coloring until it is deep orange, and use it to pipe dots on the uncovered edges of the strips with the #2 tip. Using figure **1** as a guide, outline the cherry design with dots of dark-blue piping gel. Fill it in with dots of red, pink, and clear piping gel.

To make the gold strap, roll out 2 ⅛-inch-thick cords of gum paste 15 inches long and twist them into a rope. Brush the ends with a little water and attach them to the top edges of the crust, draping the rope down the side and around the back of the cake. Mix gold powder with lemon extract and paint the strap. Finish each end with a ¼-inch silver dragée encircled by 7 ³⁄₁₆-inch ones. Place the cherries on and around the cake.

1

busy beehive

This honey of a cake in an icing cage will create a buzz at any birthday party. The gum-paste bees even sport edible wings made of sheet gelatin.

- cakes:
- – 7-inch round, 2 inches high
- – 6-inch round, 3 inches high, baked in a metal bowl 6¼ inches wide at the top and 3 inches wide at the bottom
- metal bowl, 10 inches wide at the top, 3 inches wide at the bottom, and 3 inches high
- permanent nontoxic felt-tip marker
- vegetable shortening
- pastry bag and coupler
- tips: PME #2, #5
- royal icing (page 147)
- colors:
- – brown and golden-yellow paste
- – nontoxic black powder
- gum paste (page 154)
- small knife

- 10 #22-gauge white cloth-covered wires
- needle-nose pliers
- X-acto knife
- block of Styrofoam
- lemon extract
- small paintbrush
- 40 black stamens (page 178)
- scissors
- sheet gelatin
- black food-coloring marking pen
- 7-inch round foamcore board
- rolled fondant (page 145)

In advance:

Make the royal-icing cage by piping on the 6¼-inch and 10-inch metal bowls. Invert the bowls and, using the permanent marker, draw patterns **1** and **2** directly on them. Draw the pattern all the way around the bowl. Coat the outsides of the bowls *lightly* with shortening to prevent the icing from sticking. (The best way to avoid applying too much grease is to rub your hands with a tiny amount of shortening and then rub the bowls.) With the #5 tip, pipe brown royal icing over the designs. Overpipe the centers of the flowers and some of the branches to add strength to the cage. Let the icing dry on the bowls overnight.

To make the 9 bees on wires, tint some gum paste yellow. For each bee, the body is 1 inch long, ½ inch thick at its widest point, and tapered to ¼ inch at one end (**3**). With the tip of a small knife, score 4 rings around the bee at ⅛-inch intervals. Make a hook on the end of a wire with the pliers, moisten it with water, and then insert it into the bee. With the X-acto knife, make 2 holes in the head for the antennae and 2 small

127

slits in the body for the wings. Let dry in the block of Styrofoam.

Mix black powdered color with lemon extract and paint alternating stripes on the bees, ending with a small circle on the tapered end. Insert 2 stamens in the head for the antennae. For the eyes, cut the heads off 2 stamens, leaving ¼ inch of the stems, and insert them below the antennae. With the scissors, cut the sheet gelatin in the shape of wings 1 inch long and ½ inch wide and tapered to a point (**3**). Draw the patterns on the wings with the food-coloring marker. Insert the wings into the slits on the body.

To decorate:
Bake the cakes and let them cool completely. Fill the layers and assemble them on the board. With the serrated knife, carefully shave off the sides of the cake a little at a time to form the rings of the beehive (**4**). Crumb-coat the cake (see page 150) and chill it. Cover the cake with yellow rolled fondant.

Carefully remove the 2 pieces of the cage from the bowls. Place the larger one over the cake, then attach the smaller one with brown royal icing. Insert the bees into the cake through the cage.

1 enlarge 200%

3"

2 enlarge 480%

3

4

margot's bracelet

SERVES 60

My friend Margot has an extensive bracelet collection and is never seen without at least one of them, and often many. So I thought she should have one on her cake, too. The sophisticated royal-icing ring gives this cake a grown-up look, but the candies, colors, and wired decorations bring out the child in all of us.

- cakes:
- 6-inch round,
  3 inches high
- 8-inch round,
  3 inches high
- 12-inch petal,
  3 inches high
- 16-inch round base,
  ½ inch high
- royal icing (page 147)
- colors:
- kelly-green, lemon-yellow,
  orange, teal, and pink
  paste
- yellow, red, orange, teal,
  and pink airbrush paint
- red nontoxic iridescent
  powder
- ½-inch-wide baby-blue
  ribbon
- white glue
- wax paper or silicone-
  coated parchment paper
- 9-inch round cake pan,
  3 inches high, for the
  bracelet
- pastry bags and couplers
- tips: #5, PME #2, #3
- gum paste (page 154)

- assorted cutters: daisies,
  stars, and hearts
- needle-nose pliers
- 6 #20-gauge cloth-covered
  wires, 18 inches long
- airbrush
- clear piping gel
- edible glitter in assorted
  colors
- lemon extract
- block of Styrofoam
- 1 6-inch round, 1 8-inch
  round, and 1 12-inch
  petal foamcore board
- small serrated knife
- rolled fondant (page 145)
- ¼-inch-thick wooden
  dowels
- assorted candies:
- 21 bananas, 12 limes,
  and 8 *each* yellow hearts
  and oranges
- 8 *each* yellow and blue
  and 16 *each* red and
  green jelly crescents

In advance:

Cover the base with thinned lime-green (a mixture of kelly-green and lemon-yellow) royal icing. Let dry. Glue the ribbon around the edge.

Make the royal-icing collar. Cut a strip of wax or parchment paper big enough to cover the outer sides of the 9-inch pan. Enlarge pattern **1** and trace it on the paper. DO NOT tape the paper to the pan, as that would make it impossible to get it off without shattering the icing. Instead, wrap the paper around the pan, then tape the 2 ends together. It will then be easy to slide the paper off the pan when the icing is dry. Using the #5 tip, pipe the design with white royal icing. Overpipe with the #3 tip, adding ropes as indicated. Let the collar dry on the pan overnight.

Roll out some gum paste ⅛ inch thick and cut

131

out 30 flowers with the assorted cutters. Let dry. With the pliers, bend the wires into curled, spiral, and heart shapes, as shown in the photograph on page 130. Cut out gum-paste stars, hearts, and flowers and attach them to the wires by putting a dab of royal icing on the back. Let the icing dry. With the airbrush, spray the centers of the gum-paste flowers yellow, then pipe a dot of white royal icing in the middle with the #2 tip. Spray the decorations and wires yellow and red, as indicated in the photograph. Spread the fronts with piping gel and dust them with edible glitter.

With the #2 tip, pipe dots along the heart-shaped wire. Mix red iridescent powder with lemon extract and paint the dots forming the heart, leaving the dots on the stem white. Insert all the wires into the Styrofoam block to dry.

To decorate:

Bake the cakes and let them cool completely. Fill the tiers and assemble them on their corresponding boards.

With the serrated knife, cut off the tops of the tiers at an angle, a little at a time, so that each tier slopes down on one side to 1¾ inches high. On the bottom tier, from the top edge, cut diagonally downward from right to left at each indentation on the petals. Crumb-coat the tiers (see page 150) and chill them. Cover the 12-inch tier with orange fondant, the 8-inch tier with teal fondant, and the 6-inch tier with pink fondant. Insert dowels in the bottom tier. With the airbrush, spray the bottom tier orange only in the indented areas. Spray the middle tier teal, and on the top tier spray pink vertical stripes, as shown in the photograph.

Stack the tiers on the base, attaching them with royal icing. Insert a sharpened dowel all the way through the entire cake to secure it. Use

royal icing to attach the banana candies around the bottom edge of the top tier, alternating them with the lime candies. Around the bottom edge of the bottom tier, attach the yellow jelly candies, curved side in, at the diagonal cuts. Attach the tops of the yellow hearts to the straight side of the candies, gluing them to the base with royal icing. Attach 1 red jelly candy, straight side in, then 2 green jellies stacked next to it, with an orange candy on top. Place 1 blue jelly, straight side in, in front, with a banana candy on top. Add another red jelly and then continue around the base, filling in any gaps with flowers.

Carefully remove the royal-icing design from the pan. Gently peel away the paper and place the ring around the middle tier, attaching it with royal icing. Glue the flowers around the top and bottom tiers with royal icing. Insert the wired decorations into the top of the cake.

connect A and B

1B

connect A and B

1A   enlarge 205%

terry's presents

SERVES 195 This special cake, a tumbling pile of gaily decorated gift boxes, was made for the birthday of my oldest friend, Terry. The lids of the boxes could be made of cake, but I have chosen to make them out of Styrofoam, to lessen the weight of the tiers. In either case, the directions would be the same.

- cakes:
  - 3½-inch square, 2½ inches high
  - 6-inch square, 4 inches high
  - 10-by-8-inch rectangle, 5½ inches high
  - 13-by-10½-inch rectangle, 6½ inches high
- 15-by-13½-inch base, ½ inch high
- 18-by-½-by-16½-inch base, ½ inch high
- royal icing (page 147)
- colors:
  - egg-yellow, lemon-yellow, red, leaf-green, orange, black, avocado, apricot, rose, teal, and royal-blue paste
  - nontoxic super pearl, yellow, silver, Georgia peach, and midnight-blue iridescent powders

(continued)

In advance:

Glue the smaller base, centered, to the top of the larger base. Cover the smaller base with thinned pale egg-yellow royal icing and the larger one with thinned white royal icing. Let them dry. Glue ribbon around the edges.

To make the 2 gum-paste bows and streamers, roll out the gum paste 1/16 inch thick. For the smaller bow, roll the ridged rolling pin parallel to the length of the paste, then cut strips with the pizza cutter, following the ridges. Let the bows dry.

To make the bow for the top tier, you will need 5 loops. Cut the gum paste into 5-by-1-inch strips. Brush one of the short ends with water and pinch the 2 ends together, forming a loop. Let them dry on their sides (**1**). Make 2 streamers 1 inch wide and 4 inches long. Let dry.

- lilac and black powder
- pink and yellow airbrush paint
- ½-inch-wide peach ribbon
- white glue
- gum-paste decorations (page 154):
  2 bows, one 6½ inches wide and 8 inches long, the other 5 inches wide and 6 inches long
- pizza cutter
- ridged rolling pin
- white and chocolate rolled fondant (page 145)
- egg-crate foam pad
- long needle for making holes in pearls
- dental floss
- lemon extract
- small, soft paintbrushes
- tips: #18 star, PME #3
- wax paper
- foamcore boards:
  - 3½-inch square
  - 3½-by-4-inch rectangle
  - 6-inch square
  - 6½-by-7-inch rectangle
  - 10-by-8-inch rectangle
  - 11-by-8½-inch rectangle
  - 2 13-by-10½-inch rectangles

- 14-by-11-inch rectangle
- ¼-inch-wide wooden dowels
- Styrofoam layers:
  - 3½-by-4-inch, ½ inch high with its foamcore board attached
  - 6½-by-7-inch rectangle, 1½ inches high, with its foamcore board attached
  - 11-by-8½-inch rectangle, 1½ inches high, with its foamcore board attached
  - 14-by-11-inch rectangle, 2½ inches high, with its foamcore board attached
- small serrated knife
- hot glue gun
- clay gun
- tracing wheel
- large S-shaped and small diamond-shaped crimpers
- ½-, 1-, and 1½-inch plain round cutters

To make the tissue paper, roll out sheets of gum paste as thinly as possible. Cut out triangles and rectangles about 4 inches wide with the pizza cutter and fold each shape around a crumpled piece of tissue. Make about 40 pieces of tissue. Let them dry overnight.

To make the pearls, roll white fondant into 140 balls, ¼ inch wide and ½ inch wide. Place them in egg-crate foam so they won't flatten. Let them dry for a few hours, then make pin holes through the centers of 51 pearls for stringing. Let them dry completely.

String the pearls, using a needle threaded with dental floss. Double the floss and knot the ends together (**2**). Make 3 strands of equal numbers of pearls with holes. Mix super pearl powder with lemon extract and carefully paint the pearls.

On wax paper placed on a cookie sheet, pipe 30 royal-icing loops for the large bow, using pale lemon-yellow icing and the #18 star tip. Let them dry overnight. Mix yellow iridescent powder with lemon extract and paint the loops. Let them dry.

You can assemble the royal-icing bow on wax paper, to place on the cake later, or directly on the cake. Pipe a thick circle of pale yellow royal icing with the #18 tip. Arrange the pointed ends of the loops in a circle in the icing (**3**). Pipe another circle of icing on top of the first one, making it a little smaller, and arrange another row of loops with the ends pointed downward. Continue until the bow is complete (**4**).

To decorate:

Bake the cakes and let them cool completely. Fill the layers and assemble them on their corresponding boards. There should be 2 13-by-10½-inch layers, each 3 inches high, on a foamcore board. Insert dowels in one cake layer, cover the top with pale egg-yellow fondant, and place the

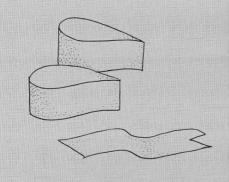

1

2

3

4

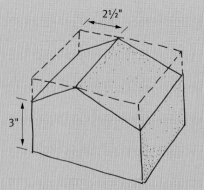

5

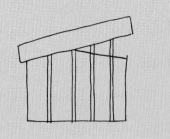

6

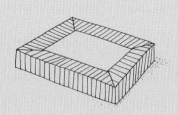

7

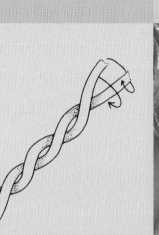

8

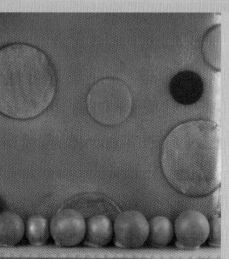

9

other layer on top. Turn the largest tier so the longer side is facing you. Starting at the top right edge, shave off the top at an angle, a little at a time, with the serrated knife, so that the left side is 4½ inches high and the right is 6 inches high.

With the longer side of the 8-by-10-inch tier facing you, shave off the top left edge, a little at a time, so that the right side is 4 inches high. Shave off the top of the 6-inch tier from a point 2½ inches from the left side so that both sides are 3 inches high (**5**).

Cut the 3½-inch tier from the top right edge so that the left side is 1½ inches high. Crumb-coat the tiers and chill them.

Insert dowels in each tier and cut those nearest the higher end ¾ inch above the surface (**6**). Squeeze some royal icing on top of the cake, covering the dowels. Add the lids, propping them on the dowels to extend ¼ inch on all sides.

Cover the largest tier with pale egg-yellow fondant to match the base. With the round cutters, cut ½-inch circles of red fondant, 1-inch circles of pale leaf-green fondant, and 1½-inch circles of orange fondant. Attach them to the side of the tier with a little water.

To make the ribbon, roll out white fondant ¼ inch thick. With the pizza cutter, cut 2 6-by-2-inch strips. Brushing one side with water, attach them to the 13-inch sides of the tier 2 inches from the corner, with one end folded ½ inch over the top. Cut 1 strip 7 by 2 inches and 1 5¼ by 2 inches, and attach them to the higher and lower 10½-inch sides of the tier. Mix lilac and super pearl powder with lemon extract and paint the ribbons and the bow.

Cover the largest Styrofoam lid and board with white fondant. Mark the outline of the tier above on top of the lid with a toothpick. Then mark diagonal lines down each corner from the marks above. Tint a piece of chocolate fon-

dant black. Press it through the ⅛-inch-circle die of the clay gun to make many cords. Attach them, ½ inch apart, from the marked line on the top down the side of the lid, attaching them with a little water (**7**). Mix black powdered color with lemon extract and paint in between every other set of stripes.

Repeat the process with red, pale avocado-green, and pale egg-yellow fondant and attach the cords between the black cords in the painted areas.

Cover the 10-inch tier with apricot fondant and its lid with rose fondant. Roll out white fondant ¼ inch thick. To make the ribbons, roll the ridged rolling pin over the surface, then cut it into 1½-inch-wide strips, with the ridges running lengthwise. Attach them diagonally to the sides of the cake, as shown in the photograph. Mix midnight-blue and super pearl iridescent powdered colors with lemon extract and paint the ribbon and bow. Mix super pearl iridescent powder with lemon extract and paint the lid.

Tint 3 pieces of fondant teal, darker blue (a mixture of royal blue and teal), and lemon yellow. Roll them ⅛ inch thick. Cut the teal and blue fondant into ½-inch squares. Brushing them with water, attach them diagonally in alternating colors in vertical rows 1½ inches apart. Cut the squares as needed to fit around the ribbon. Cut the yellow fondant into ¼-inch squares and attach them to the blue squares. Mix white iridescent powder with lemon extract and paint the teal and yellow squares, being careful to leave the blue squares exposed.

Cover the 6½-inch tier with green fondant (a mixture of leaf and avocado green) and its lid with royal-blue fondant. With the S-shaped crimpers, emboss 2 continuous vertical lines ½ inch apart down the sides of the tier. Then emboss the same design 1 inch from the first, and continue around the sides of the tier. Mix blue iridescent powder with lemon extract and paint the areas between the 2 lines. Mix Georgia peach iridescent powder and lemon extract and paint the sections on both sides of the blue stripes.

To make the rope, roll a cord of ½-inch-thick yellow fondant 12 inches long. Fold it in half and twist it (**8**). Attach it to the cake with water, as shown in the photograph. Make 3 more ropes and attach them to the remaining sides of the cake. Mix yellow and super pearl iridescent powders with lemon extract and paint the ropes. Mix blue and super pearl iridescent powders with lemon extract and paint the lid.

Cover the top tier and lid with white fondant. Cut 2½-inch-wide strips of white fondant and attach them to the front and back of the tier. Cut 2 more strips, 3½ and 2½ inches long, and attach them to the higher and lower sides. Mix super pearl with lemon extract and paint the strips and the bow for this tier. Mix black powder with lemon extract and paint spots, as shown in the photograph. Mix silver iridescent powder and super pearl with lemon extract and paint the cake and lid around the spots.

Transfer the 13-inch tier to the base, gluing it in place with royal icing. Glue the remaining unstrung pearls around the base of the bottom layer with royal icing, alternating larger and smaller pearls, as shown in the photograph. Mix lilac and super pearl powders with lemon extract and paint the larger pearls. Paint the smaller pearls a lighter shade of lilac.

Assemble all the tiers with their lids.

Roll a ½-inch-thick cord of apricot fondant long enough to wrap around the bottom edge of the apricot tier. Brush one side with a little water and attach it to the cake. With the diamond-shaped crimpers, emboss a continuous design in the border. Mix yellow and super pearl iridescent powders with lemon extract and paint the diamonds.

Roll a cord of green fondant to match the green tier long enough to wrap around the bottom edge. Brush it with water and attach it to the cake. With the S-shaped crimper, emboss a continuous design in the border.

Make a white fondant rope about ½ inch thick and attach it around the bottom of the top tier. Mix silver and super pearl powders with lemon extract and paint the rope.

With royal icing, attach the gum-paste and royal-icing bows to the cake with royal icing, as shown in the photograph. Attach the white loop bow to the top tier, gluing the ribbons on first, then the loops on top (**9**). Place a half circle of fondant on the front and back of the bow at the point where the loops meet.

With the airbrush, lightly spray ⅓ of the gum-paste tissues pink and another third yellow, leaving the rest white. Attach the tissues in the gaps between the lids and the boxes with royal icing. Place the strings of pearls with royal icing, as shown.

basic

recipes

bourbon chocolate cake

This is my most-requested cake recipe. Not only is it delicious, but you don't need a mixer to make it — just whisk all of the ingredients together.

- 2 cups all-purpose flour
- 1 teaspoon baking soda
- pinch salt
- 1¾ cups hot coffee
- ¼ cup bourbon
- 5 ounces unsweetened baking chocolate, cut into small pieces
- 2 sticks (8 ounces) unsalted butter, cut into small pieces
- 2 cups sugar
- 2 eggs, at room temperature
- 1 teaspoon vanilla extract

Preheat the oven to 275 degrees F. Grease and flour 2 8- or 9-inch round pans. Sift together the flour, baking soda, and salt.

Combine the coffee, bourbon, chocolate, and butter in a large covered metal bowl. Let stand until completely melted, then whisk together. Whisk in the sugar and cool. Whisk in the flour mixture in 2 batches, then the eggs and the vanilla.

Pour the batter into the prepared pans and bake for 45 minutes (checking after 30 minutes for even baking) or until a toothpick inserted in the center comes out clean. Cool the cakes completely in the pans on wire racks. You can then either refrigerate them in the pans, wrapped in plastic, or use them right away, though it's easier to decorate a cool cake. To remove the cakes from the pans, run a knife around the inside edges of the pan and place it over a low flame to melt the grease, making sure to keep the pan moving to prevent burning. The cake should slide out easily when you invert the pan.

- Serves 20

colette's white cake

This is a delicious and simple cake with an angel food–like taste. For variety, you can flavor it with extracts or liqueurs.

- 8 ounces *each* all-purpose and cake flour
- 2 teaspoons baking powder
- 2 sticks (8 ounces) unsalted butter, at room temperature
- 21 ounces sugar
- ¾ teaspoon salt
- 2 teaspoons vanilla extract
- 1 cup egg whites, at room temperature
- 1½ cups milk, at room temperature

Preheat the oven to 325 degrees F. Grease and flour 2 8- or 9-inch round pans. Sift together the flours and baking powder.

Cream the butter and sugar in a large mixing bowl until fluffy. Add the salt and vanilla and mix well. Add the eggs, scraping the sides of the bowl, and mix until light and fluffy. Add the flour mixture in 3 batches, alternating with the milk, mixing after each addition and ending with the flour. Mix just until combined. Do not overmix.

Pour the batter into the prepared pans. Bake 30 to 35 minutes or until a toothpick inserted in the center comes out clean. Cool the cakes in the pans on wire racks for 15 minutes. Invert the cakes onto the racks and remove the pans. Let the cakes cool completely. Wrap and refrigerate before decorating.

- Serves 20

basic buttercream

Very easy to make, basic buttercream is ideal for icing a cake and for piping decorations and borders. It will stay fresh at room temperature for 2 days and can be refrigerated for up to 2 weeks.

- 1 cup butter or margarine, at room temperature
- ½ cup milk, at room temperature
- 2 teaspoons vanilla extract or other desired flavoring
- 2 pounds confectioners' sugar

Combine all ingredients in a large mixing bowl and mix at slow speed until smooth. If stiffer icing is needed, or if the weather is very warm, add a little more confectioners' sugar.

Chocolate Buttercream: Add ½ cup of unsweetened cocoa and 2 tablespoons of cold, strong coffee.

- Yields 5 cups, enough to fill and cover
  2 9-inch cake layers

meringue buttercream

This fluffy icing is lighter than basic buttercream but a bit more complicated to make. I don't recommend using this icing in very hot or humid weather. It can be stored at room temperature for 2 days or refrigerated for 10 days.

- 4 sticks (16 ounces) unsalted butter, softened but cool
- 1 cup granulated sugar
- ¼ cup water
- candy thermometer
- 5 large egg whites, at room temperature
- ½ teaspoon cream of tartar
- 2 teaspoons flavoring (such as vanilla, lemon, or almond extract or liqueur)

Combine ¾ cup sugar and the water in a small saucepan and stir until the sugar is dissolved. Slowly heat the mixture, stirring constantly, until it starts to bubble. Reduce the heat to low and insert a candy thermometer. Do not continue to stir. Beat the egg whites in a large mixing bowl at medium speed until foamy. Add the cream of tartar and beat at high speed until soft peaks form.

Gradually add the remaining ¼ cup sugar and beat until stiff peaks form. Meanwhile, boil the sugar mixture until it reaches 248–250 degrees F on the candy thermometer. DO NOT LET THE TEMPERATURE EXCEED 250 DEGREES F. Remove from the heat and immediately pour the sugar into a glass measuring cup to stop it from cooking. Pour a little of the mixture over the egg whites and beat at slow speed. Slowly add the remaining sugar. Beat at high speed for 2 minutes, then reduce to low until the mixture is cool. Add the butter, 1 tablespoon at a time, beating at low speed until all of the butter is incorporated and the mixture is smooth. Add the flavoring.

- Yields 4½ cups, enough to cover and fill
  2 9-inch cake layers

chocolate ganache

For chocolate lovers, this is the most delicious icing for filling and covering a cake. You can use it as a glaze when it is freshly made or beat it until it becomes thick and spreadable. Because ganache is very stable, it's perfect for crumb-coating a cake that will later be covered with rolled fondant, though it will soften in very hot weather. It can be stored at room temperature for 2 days or refrigerated for up to a week.

- 12 ounces semisweet chocolate (use chips, or cut blocks into small pieces)
- 8 ounces heavy cream
- 2 teaspoons flavoring or liqueur (optional)

Place the chocolate in a large metal or glass bowl. Heat the cream in a saucepan just to the boiling point. Pour the cream over the chocolate, making sure that all of the chocolate is covered. Cover the bowl and let stand for 5 to 10 minutes. Whisk the chocolate until it is dark and shiny, then cool it to room temperature. To thicken, beat the cooled icing with a hand mixer for a few minutes.

- Yields 2 cups, enough to fill and cover 2 8-inch cake layers

modeling chocolate

Modeling chocolate can be made with real chocolate or confectionery coating, as in the recipes in this book. It is similar in consistency to soft gum paste but tastes better and doesn't dry as hard. You can use modeling chocolate to cover a cake or to make bows, flowers, and leaves.

- 10 ounces confectionery coating
- 3 ounces light corn syrup

Melt the coating in a bowl, over a saucepan of hot but not boiling water. Stir in the corn syrup; the coating will quickly start to stiffen. Stir until the ingredients are completely combined. Wrap in plastic wrap until cool. The paste will seem hard, but it will soften with the warmth of your hands when you start to work with it. You can either roll it out with a rolling pin or run it through a pasta machine, starting at the widest opening and progressing through smaller ones until it reaches the desired thickness.

- Yields about 1 cup

rolled fondant

Rolled fondant is a sweet, elastic icing that is easy to use and very versatile. Rolled out, draped over a cake, and smoothed with the hands or with an icing smoother, fondant offers a beautiful, porcelain-like surface to emboss, paint, and decorate. It won't melt in hot, humid weather and will keep a cake fresh at room temperature for 2 days. Fondant is available premade from cake-decorating stores, but it is also very easy to make at home (with the exception of chocolate fondant, which is best purchased premade; I recommend either Wilton or Bakels brands).

- 2 pounds confectioners' sugar
- ¼ cup cold water
- 1 tablespoon unflavored gelatin
- ½ cup glucose (found in cake-decorating stores) OR white corn syrup
- 1½ tablespoons glycerine (found in cake-decorating stores)
- 1 teaspoon flavoring such as lemon or almond extract (the use of pure vanilla will result in an off-white color)
- liquid coloring if desired

Sift the sugar into a large bowl and make a well in the center. Pour the water into a small saucepan and sprinkle the gelatin on top to soften for about 5 minutes. Gently heat the gelatin and stir until it is dissolved and clear. DO NOT BOIL. Remove from the heat and add the glucose or syrup and glycerine, stirring until well blended. Add the flavoring and liquid coloring if you desire. Pour the mixture into the well of sugar and mix until most of the sugar is blended, then knead with your hands until all of the sugar is incorporated and the mixture becomes stiff. If the mixture is very sticky, add small amounts of confectioners' sugar.

Shape the mixture into a ball, wrap it tightly in plastic wrap, and let it rest at room temperature overnight in an airtight container. If refrigerated, the icing will become very hard and will have to be brought to room temperature again before it will be soft enough to use. If it is absolutely necessary to refrigerate a cake covered in rolled fondant, wrap it tightly in plastic wrap before placing it in the refrigerator, then remove the plastic as soon as you take the cake out again. The icing may sweat a bit, but the moisture will eventually evaporate.

To color fondant, add small amounts of paste food coloring and knead until the color is even. Use just a little coloring at a time so the color doesn't become darker than you want it to be. You can always make it darker by adding coloring, but to make it lighter, you'll have to knead in more white fondant.

When a recipe calls for dark-colored fondant, it's usually wisest to paint the fondant after it's on the cake, since kneading in a lot of food coloring can change the consistency of the icing (and can color everyone's mouths at the party, too). For best results, use powdered colors mixed with lemon extract, or airbrush the cake.

To cover a cake with fondant:

The cake must be prepared before it can be covered with fondant. Fill the layers with the desired filling and then crumb-coat the cake as directed in the section on building a tiered cake (page 150).

Dust a clean, smooth surface with cornstarch or confectioners' sugar to prevent the fondant from sticking. Make sure you start with enough fondant to cover the cake (for amounts, refer to the chart below). Roll out the fondant with a rolling pin, giving it a half-turn after every few rolls, until it is about ¼ inch thick. Slide your hands, palms up, under the fondant, lift it up, and center it over the cake. Lay the fondant on the cake and begin smoothing it, starting at the top and working your way down (**1**). Cut off the excess around the bottom edge with a pizza cutter (**2**). You can reuse the extra fondant.

If you plan to emboss a design in the fondant with crimpers or a tracing wheel, you must do so immediately after covering the cake. The surface of the fondant crusts over quickly, and the embossing will wrinkle if you wait too long.

The cake can then be decorated with buttercream or royal icing.

The following table will help you determine how much fondant you will need to cover 3½-inch-high cakes of various sizes and shapes.

CAKE SHAPE AND SIZE	POUNDS OF FONDANT NEEDED TO COVER
round, octagon, petal, heart, or oval	
6-inch	1½
8-inch	2
10-inch	2½
12-inch	3
14-inch	4
16-inch	5
square	
6-inch	2
8-inch	2½
10-inch	3
12-inch	4
14-inch	5
16-inch	6½

• Yields 2 pounds, enough to cover a 9-inch cake, 4 inches high

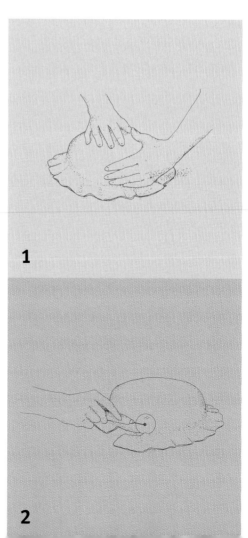

1

2

royal icing

A classic medium for flowers, bows, and delicate piping, royal icing is extremely versatile. It is pure white and dries very hard yet dissolves easily in the mouth. It can be refrigerated in an airtight container for up to 2 weeks. Stir the icing to restore its original consistency after storage, but do not rebeat it, as overbeating will break down its structure and cause it to crumble when it dries. Royal icing will soften on a refrigerated cake.

- 5 tablespoons meringue powder (found in cake-decorating stores)
- 3 ounces water
- 1 pound confectioners' sugar
  OR
- 2 large egg whites, at room temperature
- ½ teaspoon cream of tartar
- 2 teaspoons water
- 1 pound confectioners' sugar

Combine all the ingredients in a large mixing bowl and beat at slow speed with the paddle until very stiff peaks form and the icing is pure white. Add more sugar if necessary to stiffen the icing, or a few drops of water if it becomes too stiff. If you don't use it immediately, cover the bowl with a damp cloth to prevent the icing from crusting over. Let royal-icing decorations dry at room temperature for at least 24 hours.

- Yields 2½ cups

servings

The following table indicates how many servings you can expect to get out of cakes of various shapes and sizes. Since party cakes tend to be sliced thicker than wedding cakes, the numbers given here differ from those on my wedding-cake chart. This chart will also help you determine how many recipes of a cake you will need. Most cake recipes yield approximately 6 cups of batter, or enough to serve about 20 people. Each pan should be filled only halfway to ensure maximum baking efficiency. Although serving sizes will vary depending on who is cutting the cake, the numbers of servings listed below are based on pieces about 3 to 4 inches high and 1 by 2 inches wide.

CAKE SHAPE AND SIZE	NUMBER OF SERVINGS	CAKE SHAPE AND SIZE	NUMBER OF SERVINGS
round or octagonal		square	
6-inch	8	6-inch	10
8-inch	18	8-inch	25
10-inch	30	10-inch	40
12-inch	45	12-inch	50
14-inch	60	14-inch	75
16-inch	80	16-inch	100
18-inch	100		
oval		heart	
6-inch	8	6-inch	8
8-inch	20	9-inch	20
10-inch	30	12-inch	40
13-inch	50	15-inch	60

desert cookies

My mother once remarked that I would eat anything if it had frosting on it, including rocks.
She was right! These cookies are cut out and
decorated not just as rocks but also as cacti,
and even a rattlesnake, to accompany the
Just Desert cake on page 15.

- ½ cup sugar
- ¾ cup unsalted butter, softened
- 1 large egg
- 1 tablespoon finely grated lemon zest
- 1 tablespoon finely grated orange zest
- 1 teaspoon vanilla extract
- ½ teaspoon almond extract
- 2⅛ cups all-purpose flour
- ¼ teaspoon salt

Cream the sugar and butter in a mixing bowl until
fluffy. Add the egg, the lemon and orange zest,
and the vanilla and almond extracts; beat until
blended. Whisk the remaining dry ingredients
together in a small bowl. Gradually add the dry
ingredients to the sugar mixture, with the mixer
at low speed. Add water a few drops at a time
until the dough just starts to come away from the
sides of the bowl. Press the dough into a thick
disk, wrap it in plastic wrap, and refrigerate it for
2 to 3 hours.

Place 2 oven racks in the upper and lower thirds
of the oven and preheat it to 350 degrees F. On
a lightly floured surface, roll out the dough ⅛ inch
thick. Cut it into shapes following the patterns on
pages 17–19. Reroll the scraps.

Bake the cookies for 8 to 12 minutes or until
their edges begin to brown. Rotate the cookie
sheets from top to bottom and from front to back
halfway through baking. Cool the cookies on
wire racks.

- Yields 2 small, 4 medium, and 1 large cookie;
  make 2 batches for all the cookies

basic

instructions

building a tiered cake

A tiered cake is made up of multiple graduated cakes of two or more layers, with filling in between. Cakes can be surprisingly heavy: a multitiered cake must be reinforced with supports to prevent the bottom layers from collapsing. Support is provided by ¼-inch-thick wooden or plastic dowels inserted into one or more of the tiers or even, in some cases, all the way through the entire cake. Each tier rests on a separator board that supports the cake on top of the dowels.

Separator boards should be the same size as the tiers they support. You can buy precut corrugated boards in cake-decorating stores that match the size of most cake pans, but I do not recommend these because I have found they are not very strong. I prefer to cut my own boards out of sturdier, lightweight foamcore. Available in most art-supply stores, foamcore can be cut easily and cleanly with an X-acto knife.

To make your own cake board, place the bottom of the pan in which your cake was baked on a piece of foamcore, trace the outline, and cut it out.

The cake layers for the tiers should be perfectly flat, but when they come out of the oven, they are usually somewhat uneven. Wrap the cooled layers in plastic wrap or foil and refrigerate them for a few hours, then unwrap them and level the tops with a large serrated knife. A chilled cake is easier to cut because it is firmer and less crumbly.

When you are ready to decorate the cake, decide how many layers of filling you want in each tier. For example, if you have 2 layers, each 2 inches high, you may want to slice each one in half horizontally so that the finished tier will consist of 3 layers of filling and 4 cake layers. Or you can keep each layer as is to make a tier that has 2 layers with a single layer of filling in between,

although this will make the cake less stable. If the layers are less than 2 inches high, one layer of filling should be enough.

Place the first layer right side up on its board. Always use a dab of icing to hold the cake in place on its board or on the base, or to hold the tiers in place as you stack them. Then spread on the filling. Placing the top layer on the tier upside down will give you a smooth and even surface for the next tier to rest on, and will also make the finished cake look more professional.

If you are working with a tier that is more than 4½ inches high, place a separator board halfway up and insert dowels in the lower half. Cover the top with fondant before adding the second cake, then ice the entire tier to look like one layer (**1**).

Place the tier on a turntable and fill in any gaps between the layers with icing. To set the crumbs, spread a layer of thinned buttercream or ganache, using an angled spatula. This is known as **crumb-coating**. A cake that is to be covered with rolled fondant requires only one layer of crumb-coating, to make the surface smooth and level and to allow the fondant to adhere to the sides. Chill the cake for an hour or until the crumb coat is firm.

After the cake is covered with fondant, place the cake pan for the next tier on the center of the larger tier. Lightly outline the pan with a toothpick. This will give you a perimeter for the dowels. Insert a dowel into the center of the tier and push it down until it touches the board below. Mark the point on the dowel where the fondant stops. Remove the dowel and cut it at that point. Cut 6 more dowels to match the first one. Then insert these around the cake. Smaller tiers need fewer dowels, and the top tier doesn't need any support at all. To insert a dowel through the entire cake, sharpen it to a point and push it through all of the tiers and the boards (**2** and **3**).

1

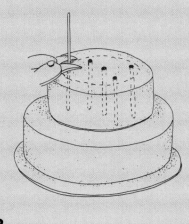

3

2

piping techniques

Skilled piping is one of the most creative techniques used in cake decorating. Many people are nervous about piping on a cake, but all it takes is some practice to feel comfortable with a piping bag and tip.

Dots: Dots are made with a round tip that may vary in size from #00 to #12. Hold the tip at a 45-degree angle slightly above the cake and apply steady pressure to the pastry bag. Squeeze until the dot is the size you want. Slowly pull the tip away from the dot with a slight swirling motion so that the dot is round, not pointed.

Snail Trail: A snail trail is a border made with a small, round tip. Hold the tip at a 45-degree angle against the cake, apply steady pressure, and let the icing build up slightly to form a dot. Then move the tip from left to right, stopping and starting at intervals to achieve a continuous look (**1**).

Grapes: These can be either made on wax paper and applied to the cake or piped directly on the cake itself. Using a round tip (a #4 tip is an average size), pipe a dot and let the tip drag to form a point. Pipe 2 more dots below and on either side of the first one (**2**). Add 3 more dots (**3**), then pipe 2 more to finish (**4**). To make larger clusters, use a larger tip or add more dots.

Overpiping: This simply means piping a design on top of another piped design to create a more elaborate and richly textured effect. The effect can be achieved by using a contrasting color of icing, another size or kind of tip, or an entirely different technique.

Stitched Piping: To make a continuous line of piping that looks like stitching, use a small tip, such as a #2. Hold the tip against the cake as you would hold a pencil, and apply pressure to the bag while moving your hand up and down and to the right (**5**).

1

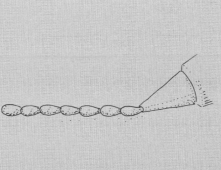

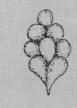

2   3   4

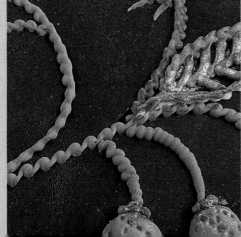

5

gum-paste decorations

Gum paste is perfect for making edible, highly realistic decorations. It can be rolled very thin and dries very hard, with a porcelain-like finish. Gum-paste flowers seem to come alive when brushed with powdered colors. Although gum-paste decorations are fragile, they can be kept for years as mementos, so long as they are protected from high humidity, which can soften or melt them.

You can buy gum paste that is ready to use, such as Bakels, in cake-decorating stores, but it's almost as easy to make your own. Use a plastic, ceramic, glass, or stainless-steel bowl; other metal bowls may turn the paste gray. Mix Country Kitchen or Wilton gum-paste powder with water, following the package directions. Add small amounts of the dry mix, if necessary, until the paste is no longer sticky. Shape the mixture into a ball and rub the surface with a little vegetable shortening. Place it in a plastic bag, squeeze the air out, and seal it. Store it at room temperature in an airtight container for at least 24 hours to let it set. It will keep for a long time and can be refrigerated, but it should be kneaded occasionally to restore its consistency.

My own preference is to use a combination of Bakels ready-to-use gum paste and Country Kitchen. I find that Bakels alone tends to be too soft and Country Kitchen alone too brittle, but the two combined make a strong gum paste that is easy to work with. Make the Country Kitchen following the package directions and leave the two kinds of gum paste separate until you are ready to use them. Then mix together only the amount that you will use that day. I use a 50:50 ratio. If the paste seems to be a bit sticky or if it's very humid, add a pinch of Tylose to keep the paste firm.

Gum paste should snap when pulled apart. Knead in some extra gum-paste powder or confectioners' sugar if it's too sticky, or some shortening if it's too dry.

ribbons and bows

- cookie sheet
- gum paste
- plastic cutting board or rubber place mat
- cornstarch
- small plastic or wooden rolling pin
- pizza cutter and small, sharp knife
- small dish of water

Cover a cookie sheet with nontextured paper towels or tissue on which the ribbons can dry without sticking. Tint the gum paste, if desired, and knead it thoroughly. Dust the cutting board or place mat with cornstarch.

To make a loop, roll out the gum paste about $1/16$ inch thick. Cut a 6-by-2-inch strip with a pizza cutter (this will make a medium-size bow). Join the 2 ends and pinch them together, making the end come to a point (**1**). Stand the loop on its side to dry on the paper towels.

To make ribbon ends, cut a strip of gum paste the same width as the loops and whatever length the design calls for. Notch one end with a sharp knife. Pinch the other end so that it comes to a point. Lay the strip on crumpled tissue so it will dry in a rippled formation (**2**).

Let ribbons or loops dry for at least 1 day before you place them on a cake. They can then be painted with powdered colors, if desired.

Before making a knotted bow, it's a good idea to start with a paper pattern to ensure that the bow is going to be the right size. Simply cut a long rectangle as wide and 3 times as long as

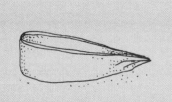

1

2

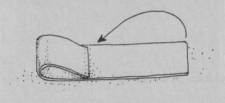

3

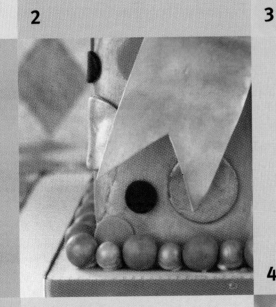

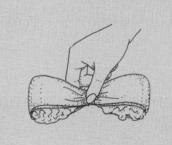

4

5

6

you want the finished bow to be. Fold the 2 ends of the rectangle into the center and pinch the paper in the middle. This will give you a sense of what your bow will look like. Roll out a piece of gum paste the size of the pattern and cut it with a pizza cutter. (For different-textured bows, use a ridged rolling pin to make stripes, or roll it in one direction and then turn it perpendicular to the stripes and roll again for a plaid pattern. Press lace against gum paste to make a lace pattern. Try experimenting with various textured rolling pins or silicone molds to achieve different effects.) Wet each of the short ends with a little water and bring them both into the center to meet (**3**). Stuff a little tissue or paper towel inside the loops to keep them from collapsing while they dry (**4**). Pinch the center together. Cut another strip about the same width as the pattern and long enough to wrap around the center of the bow. Brush a little water on each end of this strip and fold it around the center of the bow, allowing it to crease naturally (**5**). Let dry for at least 24 hours, removing the paper after about 12.

To make the ribbon ends, use the same pattern you used for the bow and cut 2 gum-paste rectangles to the length you desire. Cut a notch in one end of each and pinch the other end. Let dry on crumpled paper towels. Attach the ribbons to the cake first, using royal icing, and then place the bow on top of the pinched ends to hide them (**6**).

flowers, leaves, and berries

Gum-paste flowers, fruit, and foliage can add a colorful, creative, and *edible* touch to your cakes.

- gum paste
- cornstarch
- small rolling pin

- hard foam rubber
- small paintbrushes
- large and small ball tools
- flower and leaf cutters
- veining tool
- trumpet-flower tool
- leaf veiners
- royal icing (page 147)
- Styrofoam block
- green and brown florist's tape
- powdered colors
- paste food coloring
- liquid food coloring
- heavy (#20 or #22), medium (#24), and lightweight (#26 or #28) cloth-covered wire
- needle-nose pliers
- powdered gelatin
- egg white or piping gel
- X-acto knife
- pizza cutter
- stamens
- foil
- plastic or Styrofoam ball or egg
- tweezers

Roll out the gum paste on a smooth surface lightly dusted with cornstarch to prevent sticking. If you cut more petals or leaves than you can use immediately, cover the extra pieces with plastic wrap and then a damp cloth to keep them from drying out. Don't leave them for more than an hour or so, or they may become too dry to work with. Keep the gum paste wrapped in plastic wrap while you work.

For petals, the paste should be very thin. It should be slightly translucent, so that you can almost read through it. Roll the paste slightly thicker for leaves. Place the cutouts on a piece of hard foam rubber while you thin the edges of petals or work with the various gum-paste tools. You can buy foam-rubber pads made for this purpose in cake-decorating stores.

7

Chrysanthemum

8

9

10

11

12

13

Daisy

14

15

16

17

18

Lily of the Valley

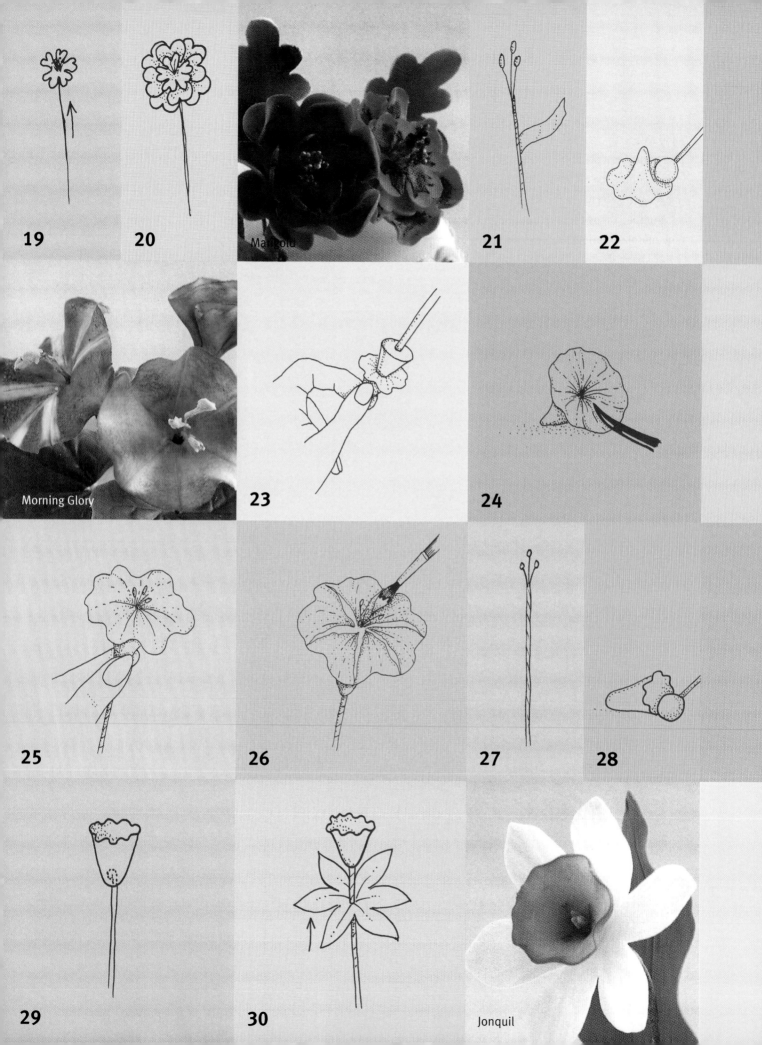

19

20

Marigold

21

22

Morning Glory

23

24

25

26

27

28

29

30

Jonquil

Roll the ball tool around the edge of petals or leaves to thin the edges and make them curl. The harder you press, the more the petal will curl. Running the tool down the center of a petal makes the petal turn in on itself.

Trumpet-shaped flowers, such as primroses and morning glories, are fashioned from one basic shape that resembles a Mexican hat. Roll a small bowl of gum paste into a pear shape and flatten the bottom with your fingers to form a brim (**7**). Place the brim on the work surface and roll it very thin with a small rolling pin. Then follow the directions for each flower, given below.

While the cutouts are still soft, you can brush them with water to make them sticky so they will adhere to other pieces of dried or soft gum paste. Dried paste will not stick with water, however; use royal icing instead.

Place the stem of the flower in a block of Styrofoam to dry. Always wrap florist's tape around the wire when you finish a flower.

Make pale-colored flowers and leaves in white gum paste. When dry, color them as needed: brush powdered coloring on the entire flower, at the ends of the petals, or just in the center, using a soft flat or pointed paintbrush. Dust green powder where the flower meets the stem and inside, around the stamens. For dark flowers and green leaves, knead paste or powdered colors into soft gum paste. Flowers can also be painted with liquid colorings to add intense dots or stripes.

Chrysanthemum: You will need 4 different-sized cutters to make a large mum. If you want to create smaller flowers or buds, you can make fewer layers. First, take a #24-gauge wire and make a tiny hook at one end with pliers. Then brush a little water on the hook and press a very small piece of gum paste onto it (**8**). The gum paste will not show; it is meant mainly to keep the petals from falling off the end of the wire.

Starting with the smallest cutter, cut out 3 flowers. Thin each petal and then cup it toward the center. Brush a little water on the inside of 2 of the petals and place one inside the other, making sure they *don't* line up. Position the third petal on top of the second and press the ball tool in the center to cup all three petals together (**9**). Brush water in the center of the third petal and slide it up the wire to the hooked end. Fold the petals around the ball of gum paste in the center to conceal it (**10**). Let dry.

Use the next-smallest cutter to cut out 3 flowers. Repeat the procedure above. Continue adding 3 petals of each size until you reach the desired size (**11**).

Daisy: Take a #24-gauge wire and use pliers to bend the end into a tiny hook. Then bend the end of the wire back about ¼ inch at a right angle. To make the center of the daisy, roll a small piece of gum paste into a ball. Wet the end of the wire and insert it into the ball of paste. Flatten the top of the ball (**12**) and let dry. When the center is dry, mix a little powdered gelatin with a small amount of powdered yellow coloring. Brush the center of the flower with a little egg white or piping gel and sprinkle the gelatin over it. Let dry.

Cut 2 flowers with the daisy cutter and divide each petal in half lengthwise with an X-acto knife (**13**). Thin the petals with the ball tool and brush a little water in the center of each flower. Slide the petals up the wire and press them against the center.

Lily of the Valley: Use a fine-gauge wire (#26) cut into 3-inch lengths and the Wilton small 5-petal cutter. For the buds, roll tiny balls of white gum paste. Bend a tiny hook at one end of a wire, wet it with a little water, and insert it into the gum-paste bud.

For the blossoms, start with a small piece of gum paste and form it into a tiny Mexican hat shape. Place the small cutter over the bump and cut out a flower. With a small ball tool, hollow out the inside of the blossom and thin the edges of the petals (**14**). Wet the hooked end of a wire and push it through the front of the flower up to the end of the hook (**15**).

To create the stem of blossoms, start at the top with the buds, using green florist's tape, and tape the flowers down the length of the wire (**16**).

To make the leaves, cut green gum paste with the pizza cutter (**17**). Vein them with the veining tool and thin their edges with the ball tool (**18**).

Marigold: Tape 10 tiny yellow stamens to #24-gauge wire. Using the small primrose cutter and bright-orange gum paste, cut out 1 flower. Thin the petals and cup them slightly with the ball tool. Brush a little water on the inside of the flower and slide it up the wire, stopping at the base of the stamens (**19**). Cut out 8 orange hearts. Thin them with the ball tool and ruffle them with a smaller ball tool. Attach them with a little water to the underside of the first set of petals (**20**).

Mix a bit of burgundy powdered color with a little water and paint the insides of the petals.

Morning Glory: Tape 3 yellow stamens to a medium-gauge (#22) wire (**21**). Shape blue or magenta gum paste into a Mexican hat. Roll out the brim very thin. Cut out the blossom with a round cutter. Thin and ruffle the edges with the large ball tool (**22**). Insert the smooth trumpet-flower tool into the center to hollow it out (**23**). With the veining tool, make 5 veins inside the flower (**24**).

Moisten the inside of the flower. Insert the wire with stamens in the center, just to the top of the tape. Pinch the trumpet part of the flower and press it tightly against the wire (**25**). Let dry. Paint white stripes inside the flower with liquid coloring (**26**).

Narcissus and Jonquil: Tape 3 yellow stamens to a #24-gauge wire (**27**). Shape a small ball of gum paste and then form it into a cone. Hollow the inside of the cone with a ball tool and then ruffle the edge with a smaller ball tool (**28**). Wet the inside of the cone and slide the wire through until it reaches the bottom of the stamens (**29**). Let dry.

Use the 6-petaled cutter to cut a flower. Thin the edges of the petals with the ball tool, then cup them slightly. Brush a little water in the center and slide the flower up the wire to the bottom of the cone (**30**).

Poppy: Press a 3-inch square of foil onto a Styrofoam or plastic ball or egg. Cut 6 circles and ruffle the edges with the large ball tool. Pull one edge with the ball tool to elongate it slightly (**31**). Moisten the elongated edge of each petal and press the petals together in the center cup of the foil (**32**). Let dry.

Shape a tiny ball of brown gum paste into the ⅜-inch-long cone for the center. With tweezers, pinch the wider end to form a star (**33**). Brush the bottom with water and attach it to the center of the flower. Attach many small black stamens around the center with a little black royal icing (**34**).

Primrose: Tape 5 stamens to a heavy-gauge (#20) green wire using green florist's tape (**35**). Shape a small piece of gum paste into a Mexican hat shape. Roll the edges thin. Cut out with a primrose cutter centered over the hat's bump (**36**). Use the ball tool on the foam to thin the petals. Press the umbrella tool into the center to hollow it (**37**), then make indentations with the veining tool from the center of the flower up the center of each petal. Moisten the center of the flower and insert the wire to just below the top of the tape (**38**). Press the bottom of the flower against the wire. Dry the flower upside

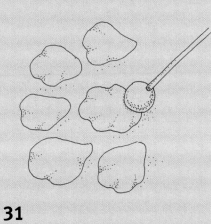

31

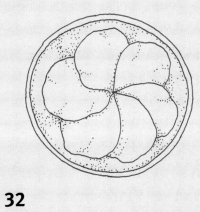

32

33

34

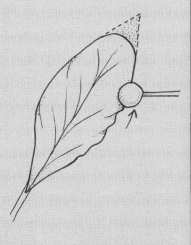

Poppy

35

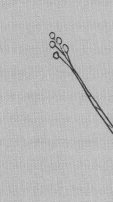

36

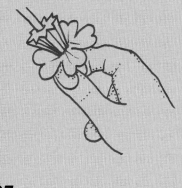

37

38

39

40

Primrose

41

42

43

44

45

46

47

48

Rose

49

50

51

52

53

54

55

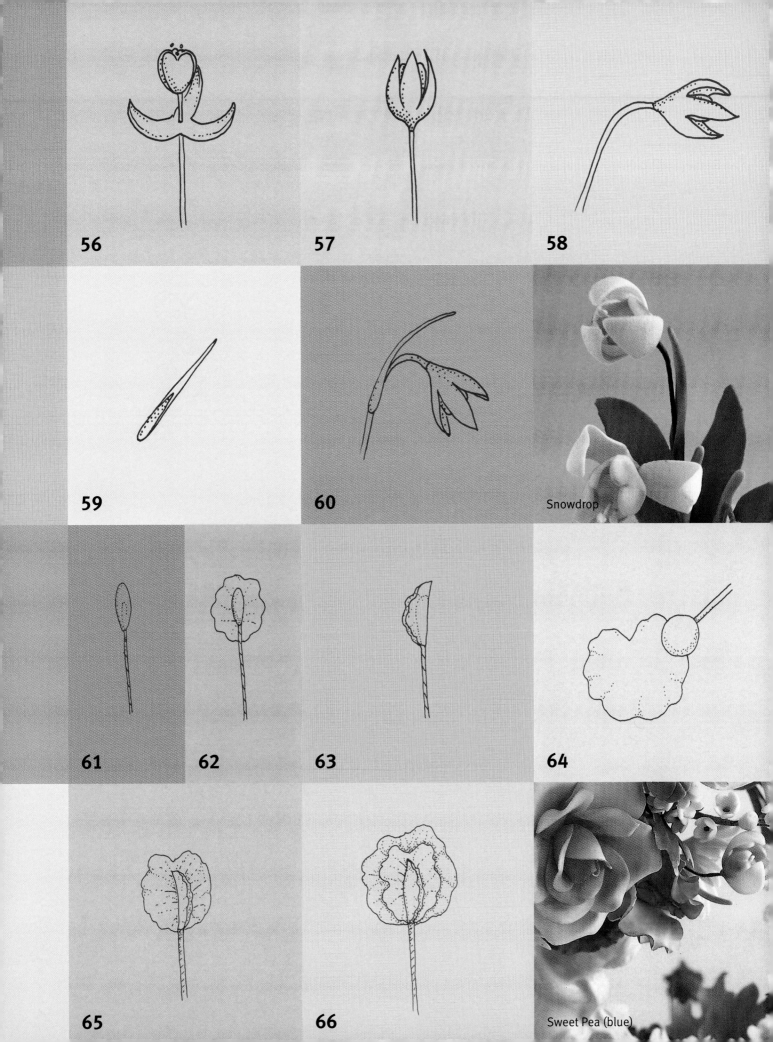

56

57

58

59

60

Snowdrop

61

62

63

64

65

66

Sweet Pea (blue)

67

68

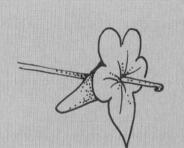

69

70

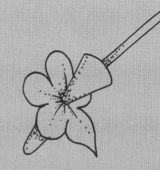

71

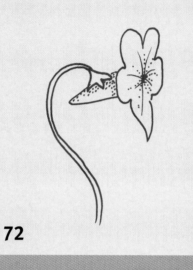

72

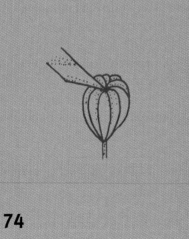

73

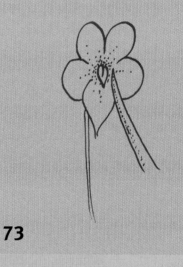

Violet

74

75   **76**

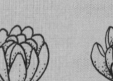

77

78

Water Lily

down. When it is dry, dust it with yellow on the inside, and blue on the outside.

Cut 3 green gum-paste leaves with the Wilton tulip leaf cutter. Cut off the tip of each leaf to give it a rounded top. Moisten the end of a medium-gauge #22 cloth-covered wire, then roll out a small cord of green gum paste, about ½ inch long. Insert the damp end of the wire into the center of the cord. Brush the back of the leaf on the bottom, about the size of the cord on the wire. Place the leaf and wire in a large silicone veiner and press the 2 halves together. The cord of gum paste on the wire will secure the leaf to the wire (**39**). Thin the edges of the leaves with the ball tool (**40**). Let dry on a bumpy surface. Dust with green powder mixed with a little black.

Rose and Rosebud: Shape a small ball of gum paste into a cone (the size of the cone will determine the size of the rose). For a small rose, use a ball about ⅜ inch in diameter; for a large rose, use a ball at least ½ inch in diameter. Make a tiny hook at the end of a heavy-gauge (#20) wire and moisten it slightly. Insert the wide end of the cone halfway onto the hook (**41**). Let dry overnight.

Roll out a thin piece of gum paste and cut a circle with a circle cutter. Thin the edges with the large ball tool (**42**). Moisten the inside of the circle slightly and wrap it around the cone to form the inside of the rose (**43** and **44**).

Make 3 petals using the small rose cutter. Thin the edges and attach them to the bud, over-lapping and evenly spaced (**45**). Curl and pinch the tips backward slightly (**46**). Cut a calyx from green gum paste and thin and elongate its tips with the ball tool. Brush the calyx with water and insert the wire through to the bud. Press the calyx against the bud and allow the tips to curl down (**47**).

To make a full rose, omit the calyx and add 5 more petals, using the next-size rose cutter. If the petals start to sag, hang them upside down by the wires until they hold their shape.

For an even fuller rose, add 6 or more petals made with the largest rose cutter (**48**).

Snowdrop: Tape 3 small white stamens on the end of a #24-gauge wire. Form a small ball of gum paste and wet the top of the wire just below the stamens with a little water. Slide the ball through the bottom of the wire, stopping just below the tips of the stamens (**49** and **50**).

Use the large primrose cutter and cut out a flower. With the X-acto knife, cut out 2 of the petals (**51**). Rearrange the 3 remaining petals so they are evenly spaced. With the ball tool, thin each petal and cup it (**52**). Wet the inside of the flower with a little water about halfway up each petal, and then feed it through the end of the wire (**53**). Press the flower against the ball so it is almost closed (**54**).

Next, using the Wilton daffodil petal cutter, cut out a flower, cup each petal, and wet the inside (**55**). Feed it up the wire like the previous flower (**56**) and press it to the center (**57**). Bend the wire so the flower is facing down (**58**). To make the bract, hollow the end of a thin cord of green gum paste (**59**) and brush a little water on the hollow area. Pinch it onto the wire just below the bend (**60**).

Sweet Pea: Make a small hook at the end of a #24-gauge wire. Dampen the hook and then shape a tiny pea of gum paste around it (**61**).

Cut a circle of gum paste. Thin and slightly ruffle the edges with the ball tool. Dampen the inside of the circle and fold it around the tiny pea, pinching the ruffled edges together (**62** and **63**).

For the second petal, use a 1¾-inch-wide sweet pea cutter and cut out 1 petal. Thin the edges with the ball tool and then frill them with a smaller ball tool (**64**). Brush water down the center of the petal, with the little bump facing down. Press it to the spine (the nonruffled side). Let dry slightly open (**65**).

For the last petal, use the other cutter to cut out a flower. Thin it as you did with the previous petal. Brush water down the center and attach it, bump side down, to the back of the last petal. Let dry (**66**).

Violet: Make a small hook on the end of a #24-gauge wire. Form a Mexican hat shape from a small ball of violet gum paste. Cut out the flower with the Wilton medium-sized 5-petal cutter, centering the cutter over the hat's bump (**67**). Thin the petals with the ball tool and elongate one petal by pulling it out from the center (**68** and **69**).

With the smooth cone-shaped gum-paste tool, hollow out the center of the flower (**70**). Wet the inside of the flower with a little water, insert the wire, and pull it through until the hook no longer shows (**71**).

Bend the wire into an S shape as shown in figure **72**. Make a tiny ball of yellow gum paste and press it into the center of the flower. Press the veining tool into the center to attach and shape it (**73**).

Water Lily: Make a small hook at the end of a #24-gauge wire. Form a medium-sized ball of gum paste into a cone. Wet the hooked end of the wire and slide the cone, wide end facing up, to the top of the hook. Press the trumpet-flower tool into the center of the cone and then, using the X-acto knife, make equally spaced indentations from the inside of the cone down the side (**74**).

There are 3 cutters for the water lily. Cut one with the smallest, then 2 with the medium, and 2 with the largest one. Thin the petals with the ball tool and then cup the petals toward the center (**75** and **76**). Brush water in the center of each flower and slide it up the wire to stop at the top, going from smallest to largest (**77** and **78**).

For the water-lily leaves, use the geranium cutter and veiner. Thin the edges of the petals with the ball tool to gently ruffle them. Place the flower on top of the leaves.

Leaves: To make leaves without wires, simply cut the leaves and vein them with a leaf veiner. Place them on a bed of crumpled paper towels or egg-crate foam to dry.

To make a leaf on a wire, roll out a piece of gum paste and cut out the leaf. Roll out a small cord of gum paste. Dampen the end of a #24-gauge wire and feed the cord onto the wire. Dampen the bottom of the leaf and place the cord on the wire against the leaf. Press the leaf in the appropriate silicone veiner. The leaf will then be attached to the wire (see figure **39**). Let dry on crumpled tissues or egg-crate foam.

gum-paste cutters

The following silhouettes indicate the shapes of various cutters used in this book. The ones marked with a * are shown smaller than actual size.

Poppy, Morning Glory, Rose center

Morning Glory leaf

Snowdrop

Sweet Pea

Sweet Pea

Sweet Pea

Deep Blue Sea

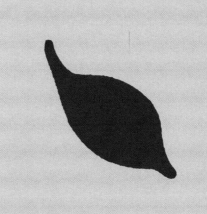

Deep Blue Sea

Deep Blue Sea

Margot's Bracelet

Chrysanthemum, Daisy

Water Lily *

Chrysanthemum

Chrysanthemum, Water Lily

Violet leaf

Rose

Rose

Rose

Primrose, Snowdrop

Violet

Cherry Pie leaf

Daisy leaf, Chrysanthemum leaf

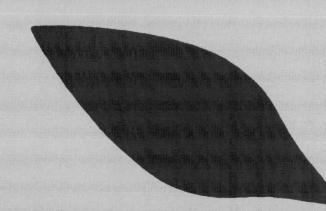

Primrose leaf

Rose calyx

Marigold leaf

Marigold

Marigold

Water Lily leaf *

Water Lily, Chrysanthemum

Gemini *

Lily of the Valley

Lily of the Valley

Narcissus, Jonquil

Holly leaf

Holly leaf

run-in sugar

This technique, in which thinned royal icing is flooded into an outlined shape, is used to make many types of icing designs, from plaques to flowers. You can also make decorations on wires, toothpicks, or bamboo skewers by laying the wire, toothpick, or skewer in the center of the outlined design before you fill it in.

To make a run-in-sugar design, place the pattern you want to reproduce on a flat surface and tape a piece of wax paper or silicone-coated parchment paper on top. Outline the design with stiff royal icing, using the #2 tip for small or intricate patterns and the #3 tip for larger designs. Place some stiff royal icing in a bowl and stir in a few drops of water. Continue adding water, a few drops at a time, until the icing has the consistency of corn syrup and a teaspoonful dropped into the bowl disappears by the count of 10. (Be careful not to make the icing too thin, a common mistake that will cause it to break down and become flaky and dull.) Pipe the thinned icing into the outlined design with the #2 tip, filling in the entire shape (**1**).

Depending on the size of the design and the amount of humidity in the air, the decoration will need to dry for 24 hours or more. I place my designs in the oven with the light on to dry them faster and to keep the shine on the icing.

When the decoration is dry, use a metal spatula or a palette knife to remove it from the paper. If you are planning to use two or more colors in a run-in design, let the first color dry before you add another, to prevent the colors from bleeding into one another. If the design is on a wire or skewer, fill in the back of the design when the front has dried.

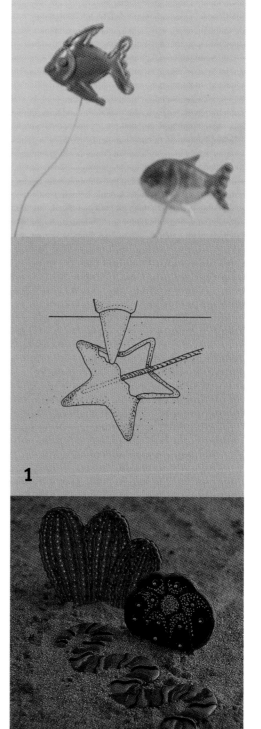

1

airbrushing

I bought my airbrush from my good friend Frances Kuyper, a master airbrusher and cake decorator who is known as the Cake Lady. Frances has been using this technique for many years and has written a number of books and articles on the subject. Since she taught me how to use the airbrush, I have incorporated it into my repertoire of sugar and cake designs. In fact, now I can't imagine how I ever lived without it!

My Kopykake airbrush is very easy to use, but many other brands also work well. The brush is held like a pen and has a lever that controls the flow of air and paint from the compressor through the tip. I use it as an alternative to hand-painting cakes and dusting leaves and flowers, and for creating shading and other effects. I recommend using only food colors specially formulated for the airbrush, since they're thin enough to prevent constant clogging. Because these colors are water-based, they make gum-paste leaves and fruits shine.

I follow a few general rules when airbrushing. First, I always test the airbrush on a paper towel before spraying something important, to make sure that the color and air flow are correct. I rarely use the compressor at its highest speed (not an option unless your compressor, like mine, is adjustable). I seldom use colors straight from the bottle, having found that mixing two or more colors in the airbrush produces more subdued shades — for example, adding a little pink to bright green will tone it down. And most important, I KEEP THE AIRBRUSH CLEAN AT ALL TIMES. If you leave colors in the airbrush, they will dry out and clog the nozzle. Cleaning before switching to a new color also ensures that you'll get the color you're expecting. To clean, run hot water through the airbrush until the spray comes out clear, or use Kopykake airbrush cleaner. Learn how to take the airbrush apart, and give it a really thorough cleaning once in a while to prevent paint buildup.

To cover a large area evenly, hold the airbrush perpendicular to the surface. Slowly spray back and forth, passing the nozzle beyond the edges of the area you're covering. For a darker shade, hold the nozzle closer to the surface; for a lighter shade, hold it farther away.

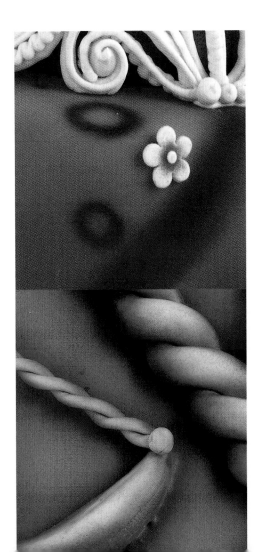

brush embroidery

This delicate technique can be used to create beautifully detailed designs on a cake. To brush embroider, you pipe the outline of a design with royal icing, then pull the icing toward the center with a damp paintbrush. It gives the design a thick-and-thin texture like that of a Wedgwood pattern. The royal icing must be slightly thinned; if it is too stiff, it cannot be brushed on smoothly. If you find you've thinned it too much, add more royal icing.

There are two ways to approach this technique. One method is to tint the royal icing before piping, which works fine for a design using just a few colors. I generally prefer the other method, which is to pipe and brush the design with white icing and *then* paint it. This way allows me to take more time with the design and to build up and subtly blend the colors.

Pipe the outline of the design (typically you'll use the #2 PME tip) one small section at a time, tapering the line at the end (**1**). Working with a damp brush, pull the icing from the inside of the line with smooth strokes so it's thicker at the edge and then fades to an almost transparent film inside. Leave the brushstrokes visible; they will give the design its embroidered look (**2** and **3**).

When painting brush embroidery, build up the colors from light to dark, as with airbrushing. I mix powdered colors with water rather than with lemon extract so the pigments can be blended together even after they dry. The water-based color doesn't set as quickly and is better for blending.

Here are some additional tips I give the students in my cake-decorating classes:

To transfer a pattern onto a cake, emboss the design into soft fondant by outlining it with a toothpick, or use a pin to poke holes through the paper and pattern into the icing.

Use royal icing instead of buttercream if you plan on painting. The icing is best if made the day before. Let it dry before painting.

Pipe the petals and leaves at the edge of the design first, then work toward the center. Likewise, pipe the background first, then work toward the foreground.

Use soft, natural-hair paintbrushes — a wide, flat brush for large areas and a pointed one for smaller areas and for making lines.

1

2

3

sugar molds

Molding a form in sugar is an easy way to make an edible container or decoration. You can use any metal, plastic, or glass cup, bowl, tart pan, or measuring cup with a smooth surface as a mold. You probably already have many containers on hand that will work quite well. (Of course, whatever you use, the top of the form must be larger than the bottom, or the mold won't come out.) Sugar molds dry very hard, and they can be hollowed out before they are completely dry to make them lighter (or to form a vase to hold sugar flowers).

To make a sugar mold, place 1 cup of granulated sugar in a bowl and add 1 scant tablespoon of cold water. Mix the sugar with your hand until all of it is damp. (Messy though it is, using your hand will make it easier to tell when the sugar is thoroughly mixed.)

Pack the sugar tightly into a clean container, firmly pressing it in with your fingers. Level off the top with a metal spatula and invert the sugar onto a piece of wax paper. Gently lift off the container. If the sugar doesn't come out easily, pick up the container, turn it over again, and tap the bottom. Let the sugar dry overnight, upside down. Don't disturb the mold, or it will crumble.

When the sugar is set but not yet completely dry, hollow it out by carefully turning it right side up and scooping out the damp inside with a spoon. Be careful not to remove too much, or you'll make the sides of the mold too thin. (You can reuse the sugar you take out.) Let the mold dry completely, right side up, for 24 hours.

painting with gold and iridescent colors

To color gum paste, rolled fondant, or royal icing with gold, silver, or other nontoxic iridescent powdered colors, use lemon extract to make the "paint." The high percentage of alcohol and the lemon oil in the extract make the paint spread smoothly and dry quickly, before the icing gets soggy. Lemon extract can be found in the grocery store. Make sure it has alcohol content written on the bottle, or it may not work.

Mix a little powdered color with a few drops of extract and stir the mixture with a small brush. To check its consistency, paint some spare fondant. If the color streaks, add a little more powder; if it's too thick, add more extract. The alcohol will evaporate, so you may need to add more extract as you work.

When you finish, set the container aside and let the mixture dry out. You can revive it simply by adding more extract.

cake bases

The base for a cake must be strong enough to support its weight and attractive enough to enhance its overall look. Depending on the design, the base should be at least 2 inches larger than the bottom tier. (This leaves only 1 inch from the cake to the edge all around.) If you plan to put flowers or other decorations around the bottom edge, make sure the base is big enough to accommodate them.

Bases can be made from many materials, including plywood, masonite, plastic, foamcore, and fiberboard. Plywood, masonite, and plastic are strong but also heavy and difficult to cut into circles or odd shapes, and plastic can be very expensive. I find that ready-made ½-inch-thick fiberboard drums with foil wrapping are the strongest and lightest choice. They are available at cake-decorating stores and come in the same shapes as most cake pans, and up to 24 inches wide. You can cover the foil wrapping with thinned royal icing to match the cake.

You can also make your own bases by assembling layers of foamcore cut with an X-acto knife to the shape and size of the cake. Foamcore should not be used for cakes larger than 15 inches, though, because it may bend. If a base bends when you lift the cake, it can crack the tiers. Two layers of ¼-inch-thick foamcore glued together should be strong enough to hold most 1- or 2-tier cakes. The wider the base of the cake, the thicker the board should be.

To make a base from foamcore, trace the outline of the shape you want on one board and cut it with a sharp X-acto knife. Use white glue to attach the cut board to a second board, then place books or other heavy objects on top so the boards will dry flat. Cut the second board around the first one so that both layers have a perfectly even edge. Use a third layer if the cake is very big or heavy.

To make a base for an irregular-shaped cake, you can use the cake pan as a template and enlarge its outline for the base. Set the pan used for the bottom tier on a large piece of foamcore. To make a 19-inch base for a 15-inch cake (for example), you will need to measure out 2 inches on the foamcore all around the pan. The simplest way to do this is to use a roll of tape that is 2 inches wide from its inner surface to its outer surface (**1**). Place the outside of the roll against the pan and insert a pen or marker in the hole. Roll the tape along the edge of the pan, marking the board as you roll. You will end up with a perfectly enlarged shape drawn on the board.

Covering the base with thinned royal icing is the easiest and most lightweight way to make the board attractive. Thin enough icing to cover the board by adding a few drops of water at a time until the icing is the consistency of thick syrup. Tint the icing to match a colored cake. Pour it onto the board and smooth it with a spatula. Let dry for at least 24 hours.

To cover the edge of the board, attach a ribbon around it with white glue. The ribbon should be the same height as the board. This will give the cake an elegant and professional look.

Use a dab of royal icing to secure the cake to the base and keep it from shifting if you have to move it.

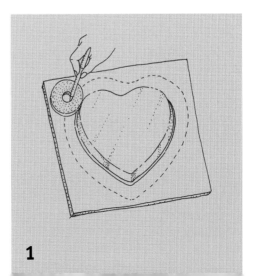

1

styrofoam

Styrofoam has a number of uses in cake decorating, from holding bouquets to standing in for cake in decorated tiers. It is available in 2 types, one with a dense, coarse texture, and the other composed of small beads, making it softer and more flexible. Styrofoam comes in many sizes and shapes, including disks, sheets, cones, eggs, and balls, which can be found at craft, art-supply, and cake-decorating stores. It's easy to cut and shape and is both lightweight and strong.

You can buy sheets of Styrofoam in thicknesses ranging from ½ inch to 5 inches. When making stemmed flowers and other decorations, I always keep a 2-inch-thick sheet nearby to stick the stems into while I work. This allows the flowers to dry upright, without becoming crushed or misshapen from lying on their sides. Transporting flowers in Styrofoam is also a handy way to avoid breakage.

Styrofoam balls or eggs are useful for supporting bouquets of flowers on top of a cake. The ball or egg is glued to a pedestal or other support and the stems are inserted into it. Royal icing can then be piped around the stems to disguise the Styrofoam and hold the flowers in place.

Styrofoam disks can be purchased in the same sizes as cake layers. Generally used for making cakes for display purposes, they are covered with icing and decorated in the same way as actual cakes. To cut and shape Styrofoam, use a serrated blade, such as a steak knife. Cut in a sawing motion, as if you were slicing bread. Cut the Styrofoam roughly, then sand it with a piece of the coarser type of Styrofoam until it is smooth and the size and shape you want. Try to work outdoors or over a trash can, as the Styrofoam will generate a lot of little shavings that will stick to everything in the room, including you.

helpful hints

- To roll fondant into a cord, you have to create friction between the fondant and the work surface. Try spreading a light coating of vegetable shortening on the surface with your hands or a paper towel. With your fingers slightly spread and your hands moving apart, roll the fondant evenly to the length needed. Brush a little water on the cord to make it slightly sticky before you attach it to the cake.

- Use silicone-coated parchment paper instead of wax paper for delicate royal icing decorations.

- When running several colors of gum paste or modeling chocolate through a pasta machine, start with the lightest color and progress to the darkest. The machine will retain some of the previous color you used, and you don't want to spoil the lighter color or have to take the time to thoroughly clean the machine until you're finished.

- To bend foamcore, score it on the *opposite* side of the curve — that is, on the outside for a concave curve, and on the inside for a convex one.

- Before using florist's tape to wrap the stems of gum-paste flowers, take an X-acto knife and cut the entire roll of tape lengthwise, so that every piece will be half the width of the original roll. This makes it *much* easier to use.

- Instead of blowing up the balloons for your next party yourself, save your breath — let your airbrush do the job for you.

glossary of basic tools

Airbrush: Used for blowing a fine mist of food color onto cakes, cookies, flowers, etc. The brush is controlled by a simple lever and is attached to an air compressor, which blows the air through the brush and mixes it with the paint.

Aluminum foil: Indispensable for piping trumpet-shaped royal-icing flowers and for forming some gum-paste flowers.

Cake drums: Foil-covered boards made from pressed fiberboard, used for cake bases.

Clay gun: A potter's tool used by cake decorators to extrude fondant, gum paste, modeling chocolate, or marzipan. The clay gun comes with various dies, which have openings of different shapes.

Cloth-covered wires: Available in white or green and in a range of thickness from #20 (the thickest) to #28 (the thinnest). Used for stems for flowers and leaves made of gum paste or royal icing. Found in florist shops and cake-decorating stores. Also known as florist wire.

Confectionery coating: Comes in disks in a variety of flavors and colors. It is not a true chocolate but can be used for decorating in place of white, dark, or milk chocolate. (Do not substitute it for real chocolate in cake or icing recipes.) Also called summer coating because in warm weather it doesn't melt as readily as real chocolate. Available in cake-decorating or candy stores.

Couplers: Plastic couplers make it easy to change tips on a pastry bag. The coupler fits inside the bag and the tip fits on top, secured by a threaded ring. All tips, except for very small and very large ones, fit onto couplers. Large and small tips can be placed directly in the pastry bag, but they cannot be changed once the bag is filled with icing.

Crimpers: Pronged decorative tools for embossing rolled fondant, marzipan, modeling chocolate, or gum paste. They are designed to work like tweezers, with the ends' embossing a design when pinched into soft icing. They come in a variety of designs and sizes.

Cutters: Tools for making a variety of shapes, flowers, and leaves.

Cutting boards: Made of smooth wood or plastic and used to roll out gum paste or modeling chocolate.

Dowels: Used for supporting tiered cakes, ¼-inch-thick wooden dowels can be purchased at hardware or cake-decorating stores.

Dragées: Gold and silver candy balls that add sparkle to cakes. They are nontoxic, but the Food and Drug Administration recommends that they be used only for decoration. Dragées are currently unavailable in California. They can be ordered from the New York Cake and Baking Distributor (see page 180).

Florist's tape: Used to cover wires and to bind flowers and leaves together. Available in brown, white, and various greens at cake-decorating and craft stores.

Foam pad: Firm foam rubber used as a surface for thinning and ruffling gum paste with ball or veining tools. Can be purchased at cake-decorating or gardening stores.

Foamcore: A thin piece of Styrofoam sandwiched between 2 pieces of thin white cardboard. Commonly used for matting posters, foamcore is the perfect material for cake bases and support boards for tiers. It is much stronger than corrugated cardboard and does not bend as easily or absorb grease. It can be cleanly cut with an X-acto knife into any shape. Available at craft and art-supply stores.

Foil wrap: Nontoxic, grease-resistant decorative paper comes in many colors and makes a festive covering for a cake base. Available at cake-decorating stores.

Food coloring: Many kinds of food coloring can be used for cake decorating, including paste, powder, liquid, and airbrush color.

Paste is the most versatile type. The color is highly concentrated; a little dab on the end of a toothpick is usually all you need to make a pastel tone. Found at cake-decorating supply stores.

Powdered food color is used for metallic and iridescent effects or to create very deep colors. Flowers can be dusted with powder to make them look more realistic. You can paint with iridescent powdered colors by adding a few drops of lemon extract. Metallic powders are nontoxic but should be used for decoration only.

Liquid food color, commonly found in the grocery, sometimes comes in handy; however, to achieve a dark color you must add large amounts, which will thin the icing and make piping difficult. Liquid paste, found in cake-decorating stores, is highly concentrated but thinner than paste coloring.

Airbrush color, manufactured specifically for use in the airbrush, is a thin, water-based liquid. Available at cake-decorating stores.

Glucose: A thicker version of corn syrup, used for making rolled fondant. Available at cake-decorating stores.

Glycerine: A thick, sweet oily syrup that keeps fondant soft and pliable. It can also be used for thinning paste coloring. Available at cake-decorating stores.

Gum-paste tools: A variety of gum-paste tools for shaping and modeling can be found at cake-decorating stores. See the section on gum paste (page 154).

Heavy-duty mixer: A necessity for the frequent baker. An upright mixer is fine for the occasional cake decorator, but handheld mixers tend to burn out and are not very efficient.

Hot-glue gun: A gun-shaped tool that melts plastic glue sticks, used to apply melted glue to Styrofoam or foamcore. Available at hardware or craft stores.

Icing smoother: A plastic tool with a handle used for smoothing rolled fondant on cakes.

Paintbrushes: Flat or round, soft paintbrushes and pastry brushes come in handy for almost every aspect of decorating. Natural-hair brushes are recommended over synthetic ones.

Pasta machine: A machine for rolling out pasta is also a great tool for gum paste, modeling chocolate, and fondant. Used instead of a rolling pin, it saves a lot of time and effort. A motorized model makes the work even easier because it permits you to use both hands.

Pastry bags: Lightweight polyester pastry bags are recommended over cloth ones, which are bulky and hard to clean, and disposable plastic bags, which are easily breakable.

Piping gel: Ideal as a clear, edible glue, piping gel also comes in colors. I prefer to add liquid colorings to clear gel for translucent decorations like gemstones. Available at cake-decorating and grocery stores.

Pizza cutter: Handy for trimming rolled fondant and for cutting strips of gum paste or modeling chocolate.

Plastic cutting board: I use plastic boards to roll out gum paste. You can also use less expensive plastic place mats.

Plastic wrap: For wrapping and storing gum paste and modeling chocolate.

Pruning shears: For trimming wooden dowels.

Rolling pin: A large rolling pin is essential for rolling out fondant, and a small wooden or plastic one for rolling out gum paste.

Ruler: Metal rulers are more durable than plastic ones, which are easily cut or nicked. An 18-inch length is the most versatile, though a smaller size can also come in handy. The ruler can be used to make a flexible straightedge out of thin cardboard when you need to mark a line on a curved surface.

Scissors: Keep scissors of several sizes on hand for cutting paper, ribbon, etc.

Sheet gelatin: Gelatin that comes in clear sheets is used to make edible insect wings or windows on gingerbread houses.

Spatula: An assortment of spatulas is an absolute necessity for baking and decorating. Rubber is best for scraping bowls of batter and icing, and stainless steel for spreading and smoothing icing. The spatula I use most often is an 8-inch off-set model.

Stamens: A stamen consists of a thin piece of stiff thread with a tiny ball on each end. The thread is cut in half, and the ends are inserted into the center of a royal-icing or gum-paste flower. Available at cake-decorating stores or from florists, they come in a variety of colors and sizes and are not edible.

Styrofoam: Essential for making bouquets, beveled layers, and display cakes. Found at craft or cake-decorating stores. See the section on Styrofoam (page 176).

Tips: There are hundreds of decorating tips to choose from. Beginners may want to purchase a basic set and buy additional tips as needed. I use small round tips more than any others. PME brand tips are seamless and more expensive than ordinary seamed tips (around $5 versus 59¢), but for certain techniques, such as stringwork, they are essential. Tips with seams tend to force the icing out in spirals, whereas seamless ones form the icing in small straight lines. I suggest that even beginners buy a few of the more expensive tips, in sizes #1, #1.5, #2, and #3.

Round tips range in size from #00 through #12 to even larger sizes such as #1A and #2A. Star tips are numbered from #13 to #35, and there are also larger ones. Leaf tips number #65S through #70 and #352; larger leaf tips are #326, #355, #112, #113, #114, and #115. Rose-petal tips range from #101S through #104 and then from #124 to #127, and curved rose tips number #60, #61, #121, #122, and #123. Ribbon tips range from #44 through #48, and large ribbons are #1D and #2B. Tips #79, #80, and #81 make mums and lilies of the valley. Besides these, there are also many other specialty tips.

Toothpicks: Round toothpicks can be tinted green with liquid food coloring to make flower stems. They are also useful for adding paste colors to icing, embossing fondant, and marking icing. Bamboo skewers can be used when longer stems are needed.

Tracing wheel: Used for embossing designs on rolled fondant, gum paste, or marzipan. Some tracing wheels have a plain edge, others have teeth, making a dotted line, and some have a zigzag edge. Available in cake-decorating and sewing stores.

Turntable: Invaluable for working your way around a cake. Cake-decorating stores sell turntables on stands, but you don't have to buy an expensive model; the plastic ones carried by most hardware stores, designed for storing spices, work fine and will support even very heavy cakes.

Tweezers: Most helpful for picking up and positioning dragées, stamens, and flowers.

Tylose: An additive used to stiffen gum paste in humid weather.

Veiners: Plastic or silicone molds that emboss veins in gum-paste flowers and leaves.

Wax paper: Used for making royal-icing flowers and for piping removable royal-icing decorations.

X-acto knife: I use an X-acto knife with a long, pointed blade (#11). The knife has a thin handle and a blade that screws in and can be changed easily. You will need a lot of extra blades because they tend to dull quickly. They can be found at craft and art-supply stores.

sources

AMERICAN BAKELS

Ready-made rolled fondant in a variety of colors and flavors, as well as ready-made gum paste.
(800) 799-2253

AMERICAN CAKE DECORATING

A bimonthly magazine that features how-to's and reader contributions.
P.O. Box 22604
Kansas City, MO 64113-0604
(816) 333-2800
Fax: (816) 822-2339
E-mail: bobharte@cakemag.com
Web site: www.cakemag.com

AVALON DECO-CAKE SUPPLIES

Ready-made flowers.
P.O. Box 170554
Ozone Park, NY 11417
(718) 835-5641
Fax: (718) 835-6830

BERYL'S CAKE DECORATING EQUIPMENT

British bakeware and decorating supplies, by mail order only.
P.O. Box 1584
North Springfield, VA 22151
(800) 488-2749 or (703) 256-6951
Fax: (703) 750-3779
E-mail: beryls@internext.com

CAKE CRAFT CO.

Cake-decorating supplies, specializing in Styrofoam dummies cut to order.
3881 Cleveland Avenue
Columbus, OH 43224
(614) 471-6105

CK PRODUCTS

Wholesale and retail cake-decorating supplies.
310 Racquet Drive
Fort Wayne, IN 46825
(219) 484-2517
Fax: (219) 484-2510

COLETTE'S CAKES AND DECORATING SCHOOL

Silicone molds.
681 Washington Street
New York, NY 10014
(212) 366-6530
Fax: (212) 366-6003
E-mail: cakecolet@aol.com
Web site: www.colettescakes.com

CREATIVE CUTTERS

Gum-paste cutters and decorating supplies.
561 Edward Avenue #2
Richmond Hill, Ontario L4C 9W6
Canada
(905) 883-5638
Fax: (905) 770-3091
For U.S. customers:
Tri-Main Building
2495 Main Street, #433
Buffalo, NY 14214
(888) 805-3444

INTERNATIONAL CAKE EXPLORATION SOCIETY (ICES)

An organization geared to cake-decorating enthusiasts, offering an annual convention in August.
(318) 746-2812
Fax: (318) 746-4154
Web site: www.ices.org

INTERNATIONAL SCHOOL OF CONFECTIONARY ARTS

Classes in pulled sugar, chocolate, and cake decorating.
9209 Gaither Road
Gaithersburg, MD 20877
(301) 963-9077
Fax: (301) 869-7669
E-mail: ESNotter@aol.com

KOPYKAKE

Airbrushes and airbrush supplies.
3699 W. 240th Street
Torrance, CA 90505-6087
(310) 373-8906
Fax: (310) 375-5275

NEW YORK CAKE AND BAKING DISTRIBUTOR

Wide selection of products and equipment, available both in-store and by mail order.
56 West 22nd Street
New York, NY 10010
(800) 94-CAKE-9 (942-2539)
or (212) 675-CAKE

PEARL PAINT

Art supplies, including foamcore, Styrofoam, and X-acto knives.
(212) 431-7932

SUGAR BOUQUETS

Silicone molds and lace presses, by mail order only.
(800) 203-0629 or (973) 538-3542
Fax: (973) 538-4939

SUNFLOWER SUGAR ART, INC.

Metal gum-paste cutters, silicone mats and lace molds, veining and gum-paste tools, and powdered colors.
2637 NW 79 Avenue
Miami, FL 33122
(305) 717-0004
Fax: (305) 717-9905

WILTON ENTERPRISES

Bakeware, decorating tools and supplies, and cake-decorating classes.
2240 W. 75th Street
Woodridge, IL 60517
(800) 942-8881
Web site: www.wilton.com

index